Premature Burial

How It May Be Prevented

Premature Burial

How It May Be Prevented

by
William Tebb, Col. Edward Perry Vollum
and Walter R. Hadwen

Edited by
Jonathan Sale

Published by Hesperus Press Limited
28 Mortimer Street, London W1W 7RD
www.hesperuspress.com

First published in 1905

First published by Hesperus Press Limited, 2012
Foreword and notes © Jonathan Sale, 2012

Designed and typeset by Fraser Muggeridge studio
Printed in Jordan by Jordan National Press

ISBN: 978-1-84391-380-1

CONTENTS

INTRODUCTION

'*We have put her living in the tomb!* The rending of her coffin, and the grating of the iron hinges of her prison, and her struggles within the coppered archway of the vault! I TELL YOU THAT SHE NOW STANDS WITHOUT THE DOOR!'

Edgar Allan Poe's *The Fall of the House of Usher* gives a delicious shiver to modern readers of the Gothic extravaganza. The author luxuriated in the same theme in another of his short stories, *The Premature Burial*: 'The unendurable oppression of the lungs – the stifling fumes of the damp earth – the blackness of the absolute Night – the unseen but palpable presence of the Conqueror Worm.' This terrifying tale, about a man whose proneness to catatonic states gives him an understandable fear of waking up six feet underground while mind and body are still ticking over, was not based merely on a phobia. To us it is a fantasy. It would have seemed far less fantastical to nineteenth-century readers, to judge by the real-life (and real-death) examples given in *Premature Burial: How it May be Prevented*.

William Tebb and Edward Perry Vollum, the two distinguished men who produced the first edition in 1896, proclaimed loudly that this was a live issue, in two senses. Both had been confronted with it themselves, Tebb when a family member was wrongly given up for dead and Vollum in person when he went through a period of 'suspended animation' after nearly drowning.

Tebb was born in 1830 in Manchester, a hothouse of radical activists. A much-travelled philanthropist and author of a book on leprosy, he also campaigned against slavery and for animal rights. Saving a fellow human being from agony, terror and suffocation in the darkness of a coffin was as urgent a cause as any he had taken up.

Colonel Vollum, a former doctor in the US Army who spent three decades working for the government, worked energetically to improve surgery, nursing and even cooking for American soldiers. Another leading light in 'Burial Reform', he more than once defied the family, priests and doctors of a sick person who gave every appearance of being in the next world, successfully dragging the 'corpse' back into this one.

Surprisingly, neither of the authors of *Premature Burial* went into any detail about their own personal cuts from the Grim Reaper's scythe. They stuck instead to compiling a vast number of cases of other unfortunate folk who had been incorrectly diagnosed as having shuffled off this mortal coil. These examples went back to before the time of Plato and new ones were still featuring in the 1896 issues of *The Undertaker's Journal*. During May and June alone of that year, Dr Franz Hartmann, a protégé of Vollum researching the same subject, received sixty-three letters from people who had cheated the coffin at the last moment. In *Buried Alive*, an excellent suvey of subterranean terrors published in 2001, Jan Bondeson declares the three men to be 'propagandists', 'alarmists' and 'credulous'; Tebb was largely ignorant of medical science and Vollum's knowledge was far from up to date. However, Bondeson gives due credit to the work that went into compiling *Premature Burial*: 'Even today, it is quite an impressive tome.'

Thanks to enthusiastic writers in *The Lancet* as well as the local, national and international press, *Premature Burial* received reviews to die for but sadly Colonel Vollum himself was to die before the publication of the second edition. (He was cremated, thus escaping any chance of waking up underground.)

His place as co-author of the second edition in 1905 was taken by a Gloucester GP, Walter R. Hadwen. Hadwen was a somewhat left-field doctor: a teetotal vegetarian, a member of the Plymouth Brethren, President of The British Union for the Abolition of Vivisection and a medic who did not hold with the germ theory of disease.

It was not paranoia but common sense, Hadwen implies, that made his predecessor as BUAV President take an extreme step in avoiding the slightest chance of being buried alive. In her will, Frances Power Cobbe demanded that her dead body should undergo 'the operation of completely and thoroughly severing the arteries of the neck and windpipe, nearly severing the head altogether'. As is described in Chapter 16, 'the solemn junction... was duly carried out by one of the authors of this work' – presumably Hadwen.

A man prepared to cut off a colleague's head was made of stern stuff indeed and the three authors needed nerves of steel to cope with the daunting subject-matter of their campaign, in the face of the opposition of many doctors who were convinced that these so-called death-like states were a rare, and very brief, phenomenon.

The second edition continued the attack, with further examples which showed that standards had not improved in the intervening nine years. The general approach to death was so casual that, according to a House of Commons committee, many burials went ahead without a doctor having examined the person in the coffin as either a patient or a (presumed) corpse. It was even worse in France, which was avoided by many as a tourist destination on the grounds that if one fell into a catatonic state, one was more liable to be pounced upon by an undertaker jumping the gun than a doctor bringing one round.

To anyone who has ever been in the presence of a dead body (twice, in my case, that of my father and later of my wife) it is astonishing that there can be any doubt about whether the vital spark of life has been extinguished. The body stiffens, the skin goes pale. Yet the material gathered by the authors shows that an apparently extinct life did sometimes re-ignite itself, as proved by those (last) knockings from inside coffins and those contorted limbs discovered too late in mausoleums. They quote the appalling case of a woman whose coffin turned out to have doubled as a subterranean maternity ward; she gave birth to a seven-month-child.

Today no hospital TV series is complete without computer screens indicating peaks of brain activity – or the dreaded flat-lining. In previous centuries, the methods to check for life involved watching for any reaction to: hot bread applied to the soles of the feet; electric shocks; red-hot pokers; and state-of-the-art nipple-squeezing forceps. Dogs were believed to offer a good second opinion about their owner's state of life or death.

No wonder the wonderfully named Count Karnicé-Karnicki found a market for his interactive burial alarm. Available at a moderate price, this consisted of a kind of peri-scope stuck down into the coffin. A glass ball placed on the chest of the occupant would, at the slightest movement, roll off, triggering a bell to start ringing and a flag to spring up a good four feet above the ground. A light would illuminate the coffin. To the further consternation of any passer-by, the lid would fly off the top of a speaking tube so that a feeble voice could croak out a cry for help.

We might hesitate to find anything droll in the subject of bogus death experiences, if it wasn't that a man undergoing this experience had not already played his own predicament for laughs. Sir William Lindsay, a humorous and bearded seventeenth-century knight, had been given up for dead. His grieving family were paying their last respects – until his grand-daughter exclaimed, 'His beard is wagging! His beard is wagging!' Indeed it was and Sir William was soon back in the land of the living.

As a jest, he swore his relatives to silence and the funeral went ahead, lacking only his presence in the coffin. The mourners were sipping their sherry afterwards when they were shocked and terrified to see him stagger into the room on the arm of the vicar. Mightily amused, he invited them to a dinner to celebrate the fact that he was late for his own funeral; a good time was had by all, especially Sir William.

Others snatched from the jaws of the grave have been less eager to see the joke. Miss Eleanor Markham, apparently locked in rigor mortis, was not only alive but conscious during the nightmarish experience of being carted off to the cemetery. Finally, she managed to alert the undertaker, who promptly whipped open the coffin.

'My God!' she cried. 'You are burying me alive.'

'Hush, child,' said her doctor, adding, 'it is a mistake easily rectified,' a remark which may or may not have been helpful.

It is extremely rare these days for a doctor to misdiagnose the condition of death, although it does happen. Exactly a century after the publication of the first edition of *Buried Alive*, a Yorkshire GP declared that a grandmother who was actually in a diabetic coma had died of a stroke. A hearse and coffin were waiting at the door. It was a policeman, attending the 'deceased' with a coroner's official, who picked up on the slight leg move-ment showing that, as with Mark Twain, reports of her death were greatly exaggerated. She was granted £38,000 as a com-pensation for her near-death trauma.

The war in Afghanistan provided an even more recent example of a terrifyingly narrow escape. Derek Derenalagi was blown up by a roadside bomb. He lost his legs and, according to doctors, his life. His body was on its way to a body bag when a member of the medical team who was washing him noticed a weak pulse. Derek recovered; he represented Great Britain in the discus event at the 2012 Paralympics in London.

If £38,000 had been paid out in the nineteenth century for every misdiagnosis of death, as it was to that lucky grandmother at the end of the twentieth century, the country could have been bankrupt. According to one alarmist theory, half of all burials were of people still alive, however briefly. There was, of course, no way to test this thesis; the participants in any survey on the subject were generally not in a position to fill in a questionnaire. It must be admitted that the cases in *Premature Burial* are in the main taken directly from newspaper cuttings and other accounts which the authors have not followed up. Some scenarios, such as the story of the woman revived by a robber attempting to remove her jewellery, recur over the centuries. This may have been because similar outrages really did take place several times; alternatively, these could have been legends and friend-of-a-friend yarns.

Despite this, the weight of evidence in *Premature Burial* proved that the problem certainly existed to a greater or lesser degree. As for the second half of the title – *How it May be Prevented* – one of the suggested solutions of this ultimate in 'how-to' books was to follow the German example of leaving bodies under observation in 'waiting mortuaries'. Here the bodies would be laid out in these waiting rooms of death until putrefaction set in or – for the lucky ones – signs of life returned. In addition, the doctors should be as well taught about the end processes of life as they were about the preceeding stages. And they should actually turn up at the patient's bedside.

Tebb, Vollum and Hadwen would be pleased to know that the misdiagnosis of the Yorkshire grandmother was an extreme rarity. Certification of death is now a rigorous procedure. Detection of death is part of a houseman's foundation year training. There is no need for 'waiting mortuaries', just mortuaries.

In terms of technology and appropriate procedures, those earlier generations of doctors may have been in many respects, like their prematurely buried patients, completely in the dark. However, some of them will have learnt that death is a grey area and its boundaries can be crossed in both directions.

Today in some open-heart surgery patients are deliberately made to 'die' or, as doctors would put it, 'undergo deep hypothermic cardiac arrest': the lungs collapse, the heart stops and the brain has as much electrical activity as a flat battery. Even the cardiopulmonary bypass pump, which normally takes over the heart and lung function, is turned off, so that almost all of the patient's blood drains from the body. Flatlines all round, in fact. Fortunately this process is reversible – at least, that is the idea. After around half an hour, the patients are revived. They have been reincarnated as themselves.

In the words of Edgar Allan Poe, spectacular as always: 'The boundaries which divide Life from Death are at best shadowy and vague. Who shall say where the one ends, and where the other begins?'

– *Jonathan Sale, 2012*

'The thought of suffocation in a coffin is more terrible than that of torture on the rack, or burning at the stake.'
– Prof Alexander Wilder, M.D.

'Burning, drowning, even the most hideous mutilation under a railway train, is as nothing compared with burial alive.'
– *The Spectator.*

'The treatment of a living being as if he were dead: the rolling him in his winding sheet, the screwing him down in his coffin, the weeping at his funeral, and the final lowering of him into the narrow grave, and piling upon his dark and box-like dungeon loads of his mother earth. The last footfall departs from the solitary churchyard, leaving the entranced sleeper behind in his hideous shell, soon to awaken to a consciousness and to a benumbed half-suffocated existence for a few minutes; or else, more horrible still, there he lies beneath the ground conscious of what has been and still is. There is scarcely room to turn over in the wooden chamber; and what can avail a few shrieks and struggles of a half-stifled, cramped-up man!'
– *The Lancet.*

'The danger, as I have attempted to show, is very real to ourselves, to those most dear to us, and to the community in general; and it should be a subject of very anxious concern how this danger may be minimised or altogether prevented.'
– William Tebb.

Premature Burial

How It May Be Prevented

CHAPTER 1: TRANCE

Of all the various forms of suspended animation and apparent death, trance and catalepsy are the least understood and the most likely to lead the subject of them to premature burial; the laws which control them have perplexed pathologists in all ages, and appear to be as insoluble as those which govern life itself.

Its Nature and Symptoms

Dr Gowers says in *Fowler's Dictionary of Practical Medicine*:

> Trance is a prolonged and rare condition of abnormal sleep, which is produced by no known external agency, is generally entirely passive, in which the vital functions are reduced to an abnormally low minimum, and from which the entranced patients cannot be aroused by such ordinary excitants as would be more than sufficient to wake them from normal sleep. They can assimilate food artificially given, and may remain in this trance condition for as long as twenty-three weeks (Gairdner), or even for a year (P. Richer). There is an absence, complete or incomplete, of sensation, and, in a less degree, of motion; and of deep and superficial muscular reflexes. The breathing becomes nearly imperceptible, it may even be impossible to see any cloud on a clear mirror held before the mouth; the respiratory movements may be imperceptible, or at least so infrequent as three in two minutes, the pulse and the action of the heart may be impalpable, though the condition of the retina will show that

very slow circulation is still being kept up. The temperature is low.

Dr Mason Good, in *Standard of Medicine*, relates a case of 'death-trance', in which a patient was fortunate enough to have her interment postponed in order to allow a *post-mortem*(!) examination to be made. On being submitted to the scalpel, the first touch brought her to her senses, and threw her into a state of violent agitation, the anatomist being almost as frightened as herself.

Conditions Influencing Trance

Hufeland says in his *Uncertainty of Death*: 'It often happens that a person is buried in a trance, knowing all the preparations for the interment, and this affects him so much that it prolongs the trance by its depressing influence. Women are more liable to trance than men; most cases have happened in them. Trance may exist in the new-born; give them time, and many of them revive. The smell of the earth is at times sufficient to wake up a case of trance. Six or seven days, or longer, are often required to restore such cases.'

Notable Instances

Many notable persons have at one time or another been subject to this disorder. In his youth Benjamin Disraeli was seized with fits of giddiness during which the world would swing round him; he became abstracted and once fell into a trance, from which he did not recover for a week.

The mother of General Lee, the well-known Confederate General in the American Civil War, was subject to trance seizures, and on one occasion was pronounced dead by the physician, and 'buried'. Whilst, however, the sexton was filling in the grave, he heard loud crying and knocking, and Mrs Lee was rescued from her perilous position and a horrible fate.

The late Madame Blavatsky[1] would have been buried alive if Colonel Olcott had not telegraphed to let her have time to awaken. Schwartz, the first eminent Indian missionary, was roused from his supposed death by hearing his favourite hymn sung over him previous to the last rites being performed, and his resuscitation was made known by his joining in the verse.

A romantic but true story attaches to Mount Edgcumbe House in Cornwall. In the church which adjoins the estate, the grandmother of the present Earl of Mount Edgcumbe was buried alive. In a trance she was laid for dead in the family vault. It was known that upon one of her fingers was a precious ring. The sexton went at dead of night, and endeavoured to force the trinket from the lady's hand. It aroused her, and she sat up.

The man fled in terror, leaving the doors of the vault and church open. Lady Mount Edgcumbe walked to her house in her shroud. Upon being received by her husband, she fainted. When she revived, she found herself in bed, dressed in her ordinary sleeping attire. She was induced to believe that she had been the victim of a hideous nightmare, and never knew the real circumstances.

The Undertakers' Journal, 22nd July 1889, relates a similar case:

A New York undertaker recently told the following story, the circumstances of which are still remembered by old residents of the city: 'About forty years ago a lady living on Division Street, New York City, fell dead, apparently, while in the act of dancing at a ball. It was a fashionable affair, and being able to afford it, she wore costly jewellery. Her husband, a flour merchant, who loved her devotedly, resolved that she should be interred in her ball dress, diamonds, pearls, and all; also that there should be no autopsy.

As the weather was very inclement when the funeral reached the cemetery, the body was placed in the receiving vault for burial next day. The undertaker was not a poor man, but he was avaricious, and he made up his mind to possess the jewellery. He went in the night, and took the lady's watch from the folds of her dress. He next began to draw a diamond ring from her finger, and in doing so had to use violence enough to tear the skin. Then the lady moved and groaned, and the thief, terrified and conscience-stricken, fled from the cemetery, and has never been since heard from, that I know of. The lady, after the first emotions of horror at her unheard-of position had passed over, gathered her nerves together and stepped out of the vault, which the thief had left open. How she came home I cannot tell; but this I know – she lived and had children, two at least of whom are alive today.'

A Physician's Personal Experience

Dr Langdon Down furnished the following interesting particulars:

The first indication of returning consciousness in my patient, who was in a state of trance, was observed when

I was reading to my class at her bedside one of the numerous letters that I had received entreating me not to have her buried until something which the writers recommended had been done. This special one was from an old gentleman of eighty-four years, who, when he was twenty-four, was thought to be dead, and whose friends had assembled to follow him to the grave, when he heard the undertaker say: 'Would anyone like to see the corpse before I screw him down?' The undertaker at the same time moved the head a little, and struck it against the coffin, on which he aroused, and sat up. On reading this aloud a visible smile passed over the face of my patient, and she returned to obvious consciousness soon after. She has not come under observation since she left the hospital.

Extracts from Medical Literature

Philosophical Transactions quotes a case as far back as 1694, of a man aged twenty-five, who slept for nearly a month. Two years later he again fell into lethargy, and at first ate, drank, etc., though unconsciously, but at length ceased doing so altogether, and continued to hibernate for seventeen weeks. In August he fell asleep again, and did not wake until November.

Another case, recorded in the eighth volume of *The Transactions of the Royal Society of Edinburgh*, is of a girl who slept uninterruptedly from the 1st July until 1st August.

The Human Dormouse

The remarkable case of Marguerite Bozenval, 'The Dormouse of Menelles', caused a great sensation for many years. The Paris correspondent of the *Morning Leader*, in a communication dated 1st February 1903, drew attention to the case, and on 29th May her death was reported in the same journal. She had been in a trance for twenty years. In 1883, when a girl of twenty-one, she had a child; and her companion, as a joke, told her one day soon afterwards that the police had come to arrest her. She instantly became unconscious, and, until a day or two before her death, she was never aroused from her unconscious condition. Her mouth and eyes were always closed, but she was fed by a tube which was inserted in her mouth, after the doctors had broken a tooth for the purpose.

Dr Charlier had attended her all the twenty years, and the first sign of dawning consciousness was in February, when her medical attendant had to open an abscess, and she started involuntarily. The day before her death, after a violent twitching of the limbs, she momentarily opened her eyes, flinched when the doctor pinched her, and subsequently asked after her grandfather who had been dead many years. She did not recognise her mother, and thought her cousin was her sister. The effort to speak and rouse herself seemed more than the enfeebled frame could bear, and she ceased to breathe at nine o'clock in the morning.

A Long Sleep from Fright

Science Siftings, 20th June 1903, says that Marie Daskalaki, a pretty girl of seventeen, is the object of a popular subscription of money to take her to Paris from Athens in the hope of getting her awakened from a sleep that has lasted for months. The history of the case is unique. The girl suffered from a chest affection, and being absolutely destitute, was given a bed in the hospital, where, when near recovery, she was so frightened by seeing a woman dying in the next bed that she lost consciousness and has now been sleeping for five months and a half. She has since been removed to her parents' house, and awakes every five or six days, but falls to sleep again almost immediately. She scarcely eats anything, sleeps with her eyes open, and appears not to hear anything. She is, however, very sensible in her waking moments, but at the slightest sound falls back unconscious.

Further Testimonies

The Chief Constable of Hereford, in a letter to Miss Lechmere, 8th December 1902, mentions a case of a girl named Sarah Ann Dobbins, aged eleven years, of 27 Blue School Street, Hereford, who died on 12th August 1879, after being in a state of trance for three weeks. The body was arranged after the manner of all corpses, and the door of the room locked for the night. In the morning the child wore precisely the same appearance of death; two young ladies, a Miss Cook and a Miss Bethel, called about ten o'clock to see the body, and it was then discovered that it had moved. Dr Smith was called in, and the girl recovered. Fourteen years later, when she was twenty-five years old, she committed suicide by drowning herself in the River Wye.

The following case appeared in the *Middlesborough Daily Gazette*, 9th February 1896: 'The young Dutch maiden, Maria

Cvetskens, who now lies asleep at Stevensworth, has beaten the record in the annals of somnolence. At the beginning of last month she had been asleep for nearly three hundred days. The doctors, who visit her in great numbers, are agreed that there is no deception in the case.'

The Hereford Times of 16th November 1901, reprints the following case from Pauillacin the south-west of France. A Madame Bobin arrived there on board the steamer La Plata, from Senegal. She was supposed to be suffering from yellow fever, and apparently died. The body became rigid, and the face ashen and corpse-like, and in that condition she was buried. The nurse, however, had noticed that the body was not cold, and that there was tremulousness of the muscles of the abdomen, and expressed the opinion that Madame Bobin was prematurely buried. On this being reported to Madame Bobin's father, he had the body exhumed, when it was found that a child had been born in the coffin. The autopsy showed also that Madame Bobin had not contracted yellow fever, and had died from asphyxiation in the coffin. A suit was begun against the health officers and the prefect, which resulted in a verdict for 8,000 francs damages against them.

CHAPTER 2: CATALEPSY

Catalepsy differs in some of its characteristics from trance, but the one is often mistaken for the other. It is not so much a disease as a symptom of certain nervous disorders, to which women and children are more particularly liable. Like trance, it has often been mistaken for death, and its subjects buried alive. It is a nervous affection, commonly associated with distinct evidence of hysteria, but said sometimes to occur as an early symptom of epilepsy. It is attended commonly with loss of consciousness. The limbs remain in the position they occupied at the onset, as if petrified. The whole or part of the muscles pass into a state of rigidity. In profound conditions sensibility is lost to touch, pain, and electricity.

Sometimes cataleptic fits are very short indeed, lasting only a few minutes. In one case, that of a lady, they would sometimes come on when she was reading aloud. She would stop suddenly in the middle of a sentence, and a peculiar stiffness of the whole body would seize her, fixing the limbs immovably for several minutes. Then it would pass off, and the reading would be continued at the very word at which it had been interrupted, the patient being quite unconscious that anything had happened. But sometimes fits such as these may last for days and days together, and it seems not improbable that people may have been buried in this state in mistake for death.

As recently as 13th January 1904, the Paris correspondent of *The London Echo* reports a case from Valence, where a young woman at the village of Fortes fell into a cataleptic state so deep that it was thought she was dead. The usual funeral arrangements were made, and the friends and relations were taking a last look at the supposed corpse when it sat up. The girl appeared terror-stricken at her surroundings, and leapt from the window to the pavement, three storeys below, and was killed on the spot.

A Reminiscence by Dr Walter Hadwen

I had a striking case in my own practice in 1895. I was sent for in the early hours of the morning to see a young girl of seventeen, who had spent practically the whole of the previous day in Wells Cathedral listening to the music and singing in some special services, driving afterwards some fifteen miles across country to the Somersetshire village where she lived. On arrival at the house I was informed by the weeping relatives that I was too late; she was dead. The poor girl had fallen in a swoon, whilst sitting in a chair, soon after arrival home, and though every effort had been made to rouse her they all proved ineffectual; even then I heard her distracted friends shouting her name in her ears without effect.

I found the patient lying with closed eyes, pale and corpse-like, upon the bed; breathing was practically imperceptible; and the pulse, scarcely distinguishable, was nevertheless small and rapid. I had lifted the wrist from the bed in order to examine the pulse, and was struck by the fact that upon releasing it the forearm remained suspended and continued in a state of suspension for some considerable time. I then put other limbs in various positions, placed the body in absurd postures, when, to the amazement of the onlookers, such positions were maintained, and apparently would have been maintained indefinitely. She remained in this condition six days; her friends, one and all, failed in their efforts to arouse her, or to gain any response to their calls. Urine and faeces passed involuntarily.

She lived four miles from my residence, and therefore I could only see her morning and evening; and a strange fact was that although her relatives could make no impression upon her senses, I could, by speaking to her in a commanding voice, get her to swallow milk from a feeding cup. The cataleptic condition continued throughout; the arms and legs would remain in the most tiring positions in which I could place them for far longer periods than they could possibly have been sustained in health.

At the close of the sixth day profuse menstruation supervened, and I noticed slight signs of consciousness. I told her to sit up, and she did so, and opened her eyes vacantly. I left the room for her friends to dress her, and on returning later I conversed with her, and found her quite oblivious of all that had taken place, but she spoke freely of the music and singing, that is, up to the point where consciousness had been interrupted. At no time subsequently had she any recollection of these six days which formed a period of such intense anxiety to her friends. I had not at that time become interested in the subject of premature burial, but many in the district, who had been excited by the sensational event, remarked that under other circumstances the result might have been of a more serious character. I could not but agree with their conclusions.

CHAPTER 3: HUMAN HIBERNATION

Dr George Moore observes that, 'A state of the body is certainly sometimes produced (in man) which is nearly analogous to the torpor of the lower animals.'

A remarkable case, resting upon good authority, illustrative of the maintenance of life under a partial suspension of the action of the heart and lungs, is that of Colonel Townshend, who appears to have possessed the power of voluntarily dying, i.e., of so suspending the heart's action that no pulsation could be felt. The longest period in which he remained in this inanimate state was about half an hour, when active life became slowly re-established without any volition or consciousness on his part. No doubt respiration and circulation were feebly continued at intervals in this exceptional case, although so slightly as to be imperceptible, or to be indicated only by pulsation of the radial artery, or by the hand placed over the region of the heart. The stethoscope had not then been invented; there are cases, however, on record, where even the stethoscope in suspended animation has failed to elicit evidence of movement. In a hibernating animal, though apparently dead, circulation and respiration are, of course, still maintained, but are reduced to a minimum. For instance, Boncleut found, in his experiments on the marmot or mountain rat, that the pulsations of the heart, which were ninety when the animal was in an active state, were reduced to eight or ten in a minute when it was in the torpid state. When Colonel Townshend died (he really died nine hours after one of these experiments), nothing could be detected post-mortem to account for the extraordinary power which he possessed over the action of the heart.

Dr Hem Chunder Sen, of Delhi, had the opportunity of examining a venerable and learned fakir who possesses the power of self-induced trance, which really amounts to a suspension of life, being undistinguishable from death. In the month of December 1895, he passed into and remained in this condition for twenty days. The fakir was seated on a couch Buddhist fashion, the feet turned towards the stomach, in the attitude of meditation, in a small but comfortable house near the entrance to the beautiful public gardens of that city. On several occasions the experiment has been conducted under test conditions. While passing into a state of hibernation, the pulse beat slower and slower until it ceased to beat at all. The stethoscope was applied to the heart by the doctor, who failed to detect the slightest motion. The fakir, covered with a white shroud, was placed in a small subterraneous cell built of masonry, measuring about six feet by six feet, of rotund structure. The door was closed and locked, and the lock sealed with Dr Sen's private seal and with that of Mr Dhanna Tal, the magistrate of the city; the flap door leading to the vault was also carefully fastened.

At the expiration of thirty-three days the cell was opened, and the fakir was found just where he was placed, but with a death-like appearance, the limbs having become stiff as in rigor mortis. He was brought from the vault, and the mouth was rubbed with honey and milk, and the body and joints massaged with oil. In the evening manifestations of life were exhibited, and the fakir was fed with a spoonful of milk. The next day he was given a little juice of pulses known as *dal*, and in three days he was able to eat bread and milk, his normal diet. These cases are well known both at Delhi and at Jaypur, and the facts have never been disputed.

Strange Fakir Feats

The Medical Times of 11th May 1850 contains a communication from a General in the Indian service who was an eye-witness when a fakir was buried several feet in the earth, under vigilant inspection, and a watch was set, so that no one could communicate with him; and to make the matter doubly sure, corn was sown upon the grave, and during the time the man was buried it vegetated and grew to the height of several inches. He lay there forty-two days. The gentleman referred to passed the place many times during his burial, saw the growing corn, and was also present at his disinterment.

Buried Alive at the Royal Aquarium

A case of induced trance and experimental burial, not unlike that of the Indian fakirs referred to, was reported in the *London Daily Chronicle*, 14th March 1896. The experiment was carried out under test conditions.

> After being entombed for six days in a hypnotic trance, Alfred Wootton was dug up and awakened at the Royal Aquarium (Westminster), on Saturday night in the presence of a crowd of interested spectators. Wootton was hypnotised on Monday by Professor Fricker, and consigned to his voluntary grave, nine feet deep, in view of the audience, who sealed the stout casket or coffin in which the subject was immured. Seven or eight feet of earth were then shovelled upon the body, a shaft being left open for the necessary respiration, and in order that the public might be able to see the man's face during the week.

He had previously been in a trance for a week in Glasgow, under Professor Fricker's experienced hands, so was not altogether new to the business; but he is the first to be 'buried alive' by way of amusement. To the uninitiated the whole thing was gruesome in the extreme, and this particular form of entertainment certainly cannot be commended. Before being covered in, Wootton's nose and ears were stopped with wax, which was removed before he was revived on Saturday.

Of course, too, the patient was out of reach of the operator, and no suspicion of continuous hypnotising could rest upon the professor. No nourishment could be supplied for the same reason, though the man's lips were occasionally moistened by means of a damp sponge on the end of a rod, and no record of temperature or respiration could be kept. A good many people witnessed the digging up process, and the awakening took place in the concert room, whither the casket and its burden were conveyed. The professor was not long in arousing his subject, after electric and other tests had been applied to convince the audience that the man was perfectly insensible to pain and everything else. Indeed, a large needle was run through the flesh on the back of the hand without any effect whatever.

The first thing on regaining consciousness that Wootton said was that he could not see, and then he asked for drink – milk, and subsequently a little brandy, being supplied. As soon as possible the patient was lifted out of his box, and with help was quickly able to walk about the platform. He complained of considerable stiffness of the limbs, and was undoubtedly weak, but otherwise seemed none the worse for his remarkable retirement from active life, and abstention from food for nearly a week.

CHAPTER 4:
HOW GRAVEYARDS TELL THEIR TALE

-

A Gravestone and Its Story

According to the inscription (now obliterated) on the grave in the Cemetery, Basingstoke, Hants, Madam Blunden was buried alive. The following narrative appears in *The Uncertainty of the Signs of Death*, by surgeon M. Cooper, London, 1746:

At Basingstoke, in Hampshire, not many years ago, a gentlewoman of character and fortune was taken ill, and, to all appearances, died, while her husband was on a journey to London. A messenger was forthwith dispatched to the gentleman, who returned immediately, and ordered everything for her decent interment. Accordingly, on the third day after her supposed decease, she was buried in Holy Ghost Chapel, at the outside of the town, in a vault belonging to the family, over which there is a school for poor children, endowed by a charitable gentleman in the reign of Edward VI.

It happened the next day that the boys, while they were at play, heard a noise in the vault, and one of them ran and told his master, who, not crediting what he said, gave him a box on the ear and sent him about his business; but, upon the other boys coming with the same story, his curiosity was awakened, so that he sent immediately for the sexton, and opened the vault and the lady's coffin, where they found her just expiring. All possible means were used to recover her to life, but to no purpose, for she, in her agony, had bit the nails off her fingers, and tore her face and head to that degree, that, notwithstanding all the care that was taken of her, she died in a few hours in inexpressible torment.

Noises from the Tomb

The Sunday Times, London, 30th December 1838, contains the following:

A frightful case of premature interment occurred not long since, at Tonneins, in the Lower Garonne. The victim, a man in the prime of life, had only a few shovelfuls of earth thrown into his grave, when an indistinct noise was heard to proceed from his coffin. The grave-digger, terrified beyond description, instantly fled to seek assistance, and some time elapsed before his return, when the crowd, which had by this time collected in considerable numbers round the grave, insisted on the coffin being opened. As soon as the first boards had been removed, it was ascertained, beyond a doubt, that the occupant had been interred alive.

His countenance was frightfully contracted with the agony he had undergone; and, in his struggles, the unhappy man had forced his arms completely out of the winding sheet, in which they had been securely enveloped. A physician, who was on the spot, opened a vein, but no blood flowed. The sufferer was beyond the reach of art.

From the *Daily Telegraph*, 18th January 1889:

A gendarme was buried alive the other day in a village near Grenoble. The man had become intoxicated on potato brandy, and fell into a profound sleep. After twenty hours passed in slumber, his friends considered him to be dead, particularly as his body assumed the usual rigidity of a corpse. When the sexton, however, was lowering the remains of the ill-fated gendarme into the grave, he heard moans and knocks proceeding from the interior. He immediately bored holes in the sides of the coffin, to let in air, and then knocked off the lid. The gendarme had, however, ceased to live, having horribly mutilated his head in his frantic but futile efforts to burst his coffin open.

The Undertakers' Journal, 22nd September 1893:

A shocking occurrence is reported from Cesa, a little village near Naples. A woman living at that place was recently seized with sudden illness. A doctor who was called certified that the woman was dead, and the body was consequently placed in a coffin, which was deposited in the watch-house of the local cemetery. Next day an old woman passing close to the cemetery thought she heard smothered cries proceeding from the watch-house. The family was informed, but when the lid of the coffin was forced off a shocking spectacle presented itself to the gaze of the horrified villagers. The wretched woman had turned on her side, and the position of her arm showed that she had made a desperate effort to raise the lid. The eldest son, who was among the persons who broke open the coffin, received such a shock that he died three days later.

From *The London Echo*, 6th October 1894:

A story of a horrible nature comes from St Petersburg in connection with the interment, near that city, of a peasant girl named Antonova. She had presumably died, and in due course the funeral took place. After the service at the cemetery, the grave-diggers were startled by sounds of moaning proceeding from the coffin. Instead, however, of instantly breaking it open, they rushed off to find a doctor, and when he and some officials arrived and broke open the shell, the unhappy inmate was already the corpse she had been supposed to be a day earlier. It was evident, however, that no efforts could have saved life at the last moment. The body was half-turned in the coffin, the left hand, having escaped its bandages, being under the cheek.

A writer in the *Referee*, 19th May 1901, makes the following statement:

I once, in my childhood's days, saw a man who had been buried alive in the churchyard attached to St Paul's Church, Deptford. It was at the period of the terrible cholera visitation which occurred, as near as I can remember, about fifty years ago. The burial had proceeded as far as the dirt being sprinkled on the coffin when the bystanders thought they heard a noise proceeding from it. The coffin was quickly raised, and it was found that the man had torn the nails of his hands and feet off in his endeavours to get out. He was taken into my father's house, The Pilot, a public-house now known by another sign, where he was promptly attended to. I saw him about Deptford for years after.

Presentiments and their Realization

Mr Oscar F. Shaw, Attorney-at-Law, 145 Broadway, New York, furnished us with particulars of the following case, of which he had personal knowledge:

In or about the year 1851, Virginia Macdonald, who up to that time had lived with her father in Catherine Street, in the City of New York, apparently died, and was buried in Greenwood Cemetery, Brooklyn, N.Y.

After the burial her mother declared her belief that the daughter was not dead when buried, and persistently asserted her belief. The family tried in various ways to assure the mother of the death of her daughter, and even resorted to ridicule for that purpose; but the mother insisted so long and so strenuously that her daughter was buried alive, that finally the family consented to have the body taken up, when, to their horror, they discovered the body lying on the side, the hands badly bitten, and every indication of a premature burial.

The *Daily Express* of 15th June 1903 cites a horrible case, from its Paris correspondent, of a boy buried alive:

A ghastly incident is reported from Benevent, where a boy, fourteen years of age, was taken ill, and three days ago was declared to be dead. The mother went almost mad with grief, and force had to be used to get the body from her for interment, asserting that her son was not dead. The day after the funeral she was discovered to have reopened the grave, removing the earth with her hands, and to prove to her that her son was really dead when buried, the sexton opened the coffin. It was then found that the boy, whose body was frightfully contorted, had actually been suffocated in the coffin.

The following remarkable case of waking in the grave is reported in *The Undertakers' Journal*, 22nd August 1889:

A lady residing at Derbisch near Kolin, in Bohemia, where she owned considerable property, was buried last week, after a brief illness, in the family vault at the local cemetery. Four days afterwards her granddaughter was interred in the same place, but as the stone slab covering the aperture was removed, the bystanders were horrified to see that the lid of the coffin below had been raised, and that the arm of the corpse was protruding. It was ascertained eventually that the unfortunate lady, who was supposed to have died of heart disease, had been buried alive. She had evidently recovered consciousness for a few minutes, and had found strength enough to burst open her coffin. The authorities are bent on taking measures of the utmost severity against those responsible.

The Undertakers' Journal, 22nd July 1890:

A horrible story comes from Mantua. The body of a woman, named Lavrinia Merli, a peasant, who was supposed to have died from hysterics, was placed in a vault on Thursday, 3rd July. On Saturday evening it was found that the woman had regained consciousness, had torn her grave-clothes in her struggles, had turned completely over in the coffin, and had given birth to a seven-month-old child. Both mother and child were dead when the coffin was opened for the last time.

Exhumed Without an Order

The following case, published in *The Spectator*, 19th October 1895, is instructive in that the victim was exhumed without an order from the Home Secretary, or waiting for any formalities, and was restored to life:

Sir, Apropos of your article and the correspondence about being buried alive, in *The Spectator* of 28th September, the enclosed may interest you. It is an extract which I have copied today out of a letter to a neighbour of mine from his brother in Ireland, dated 6th October 1895: 'About three weeks ago, our kitchen-maid asked leave to go away for two or three days to see her mother, who was dying. She came back again on a Friday or Saturday, saying her mother was dead and buried. She, it seems, had told the doctor on her way back here that it struck her that her mother had never got stiff after death, and she could not help thinking it was very odd; and it made her very uncomfortable. He never said a word; and the kitchen-maid heard nothing until on Wednesday she got a letter saying her mother had been dug up, and was alive and getting all right. So she went up to see her, and sure enough there she was 'right enough', having got out of her trance, and knowing nothing about being in her grave from Saturday till Tuesday. Luckily, she did not 'come to' until she had been taken out of her coffin. It was a 'rum go' altogether. They say exactly the same thing happened to a sister of hers who is now alive and well.

The Evidence of Undertakers

The Undertakers' Journal, 22nd July 1889, relates the following case:

Until about forty years ago a noted family of Virginia pre-served a curious custom, which had been religiously ob-served for more than a century. Over a hundred years ago a member of the family died, and, upon being exhumed, was found to have been buried alive. From that time until about 1850, every member of the family, man, woman, or child, who died, was stabbed in the heart with a knife in the hands of the head of the house. The reason for the cessation of this custom was that in 1850 or thereabouts, a beautiful young girl was supposed to be dead, the knife was plunged into her bosom, when she gave vent to a fearful scream and died. She had merely been in a trance. The incident broke her father's heart, and in a fit of remorse he killed himself not long afterwards.

There are many families in the United States who, when any of their number dies, insist that an artery be opened to determine whether life has fled or not.

Dr Chew's Reminiscences

While in India, in the early part of the year 1896, Dr Roger S. Chew, of Calcutta, who, having been laid out for dead, and narrowly escaped living sepulture, has had the best reasons for studying the subject, gave me particulars of the following cases.

Frank Lascelles, aged thirty-two years, was seated at break-fast with a number of us young fellows, and was in the middle of a burst of hearty laughter when his head fell for-ward on his plate and he was 'dead'. As there was a distinct history of cardiac disease in his family, while he himself had frequently been treated for valvular disease of the heart, he was alleged to have 'died' of cardiac failure, and was duly interred in the Coonor Cemetery. Some six months later, permission was obtained to remove his remains to St John's Churchyard in Ootacamund.

The coffin was exhumed, and, as a 'matter of form', the lid removed to identify the resident, when, to the horror of the lookers-on, it was noticed that, though mummification had taken place, there had been a fearful struggle underground, for the body, instead of being on its back as it was when first coffined, was *lying on its face*, with its arms and legs drawn up as close as the confined space would permit. His trousers (a perfectly new pair) were burst at the left knee, while his shirt-front was torn to ribbons and bloodstained, and the wood of that portion of the coffin immediately below his mouth was stained a deep reddish-brown-black (*blood*).

Old Dr Donaldson, whom we were all very fond of, tried to explain matters by saying that the jolting of the coffin on its way to the cemetery had overturned the body, and that the blood stains on the shirt and wood were the natural result of blood flowing (i.e., oozing) out of the mouth of the corpse as it lay face downwards. A nice theory, but scarcely a probable one, as all the jolting in creation could not possibly turn a corpse over in an Indian coffin, which is so built that there is scarcely two inches spare space over any portion of the contained body, and unless the supposed corpse regained consciousness and exerted *considerable* force, it could not possibly turn round in its *narrow* casket.

Mary Norah Best, aged seventeen years, an adopted daughter of Mrs C. A. Moore, *née* Chew, 'died' of cholera, and was entombed in the Chews' vault in the old French cemetery at Calcutta. The certifying surgeon was a man who would have benefited by her death, and had twice (though ineffectually) attempted to put an end to her adopted mother, who fled from India to England after the second attempt on her life, but, unfortunately, left the girl behind. When Mary 'died' she was put into a pine coffin, the lid of which was *nailed*, not screwed, down. In 1881, ten years or so later, the vault was unsealed to admit the body of Mrs Moore's brother, J. A. A. Chew.

On entering the vault, the undertaker's assistant and I found the lid of Mary's coffin on the floor, while the position of the skeleton (half in, half out of the coffin, and an ugly gash across the right parietal bone) *plainly* showed that after being entombed Mary awoke from the trance, struggled violently till she wrenched the lid off her coffin, when she either fainted away with the strain of the effort in bursting open her casket, and while falling forward over the edge of her coffin struck her head against the masonry shelf, and died almost immediately; or, worse still as surmised from some of her clothing which was found hanging over the edge of the coffin, and the position of her right hand, the fingers of which were bent and close to where her throat would have been had the flesh not rotted away, she recovered consciousness, fought for life, forced her coffin open, and sitting up in the pitchy darkness of the vault went mad with fright, tore her clothes off, tried to throttle herself, and banged her head against the masonry shelf until she fell forward senseless and dead.

The *New York Herald* (Paris), 24th January 1897, says:

Dr Good has not the slightest doubt that premature burial may take place on the battlefield, and cited a case which was afterwards confirmed by Dr Halsterd Boyland, who was present at the time, and under whose eyes 'the dead man' came to life. Dr Good continues: 'About four o'clock in the afternoon on 14th August 1870, at the battle of Borny, near Metz, I saw a shell burst over the head of a *tirailleur*[2] posted about thirty yards to the right, and in front of me he fell to the ground dead. At midnight, in going over the field again to search for any wounded that might have been overlooked, I chanced to pass by that same spot, and put my lantern to the man's face; his eyes were open and bloodshot, and from the nostrils and mouth had oozed a bloody froth. I turned the head to the right and left to see where the shell had struck, but not a scratch anywhere, and the body neither rigid nor cold. I then ordered the *infirmiers*[3] to put the man on a stretcher and carry him to the little church where my temporary ambulance was established. What was my surprise when Dr Boyland, who was then assistant surgeon-major in the same ambulance, came at four o'clock in the morning to tell me that my dead man had come to life again and asked: "*à boire?*"

'Six weeks later that soldier, Martin, was sent back to his regiment fit for service. Here the concussion of the brain had caused inhibition of all the functions; there was no heart-beat perceptible nor any sign of respiration, and if the *sapeurs*[4] had come, as they sometimes did in the middle of the night instead of early next morning to bury the dead, this poor devil would have been thrown alive in the *fosse commune*[5].'

A correspondent in the *Guernsey Star*, of 16th December 1902, writes as follows:

Some years since, a pensioner from the army worked for my father. This ex-soldier had served in the Peninsular wars, Crimean, Indian, African. In one sanguinary battle he was badly wounded, and picked up and laid on a heap with many others who were supposed to be dead. A big trench was prepared, and when ready the huge mass of dead bodies was removed into it. But now and again a body was found to be still alive. The person of whom I write was one of them. His opinion was that the hurried burial of soldiers means the suffocating in the earth of many who would recover from their wounds and loss of blood if given the chance. Doubtless in the late war in Africa many have been buried who were simply in a state of trance.

Dr Chew narrated the following circumstance:

Shortly after the Afghan war of 1878, Surgeon-Major T. Barnwell and I were told off to take a large number of time-expired men, invalids, and wounded, to Deolali on their way to England. Some of the wounded were in a very critical state, necessitating great care: one man in particular, Trooper Holmes, of the 10th Hussars, who had an ugly bullet-wound running along his left thigh and under the groin.

Our only means of transport for these poor fellows was the 'palki' or 'doolie' carried by four bearers at a curious swinging pace. When we got to Nowshera, Holmes seemed on a fair way to recovery, but the swinging of the doolie seemed too much for him, and he grew weaker day by day till we could not rouse him to take some nourishment before starting on the march, and to all appearance he seemed perfectly dead; but as there was neither the time nor convenience to hold a post-mortem, we carried the body on to Rawalpindi rest camp, where we laid him on the floor of the mortuary tent and covered him over with a tarpaulin.

This was his salvation, as next morning (i.e., the third day succeeding his 'death'), when we raised the tarpaulin to hold the post-mortem, some hundreds of field mice (these tracts are noted for them) rushed out, and we noticed that Holmes was breathing, though very slowly with five or six respirations to the minute and there were a few teeth marks where the mice had attacked his calves. To prevent a relapse by the jolting on further marches, we handed him over to the station hospital staff, who pulled him round, and then forwarded him to the headquarters of his regiment at Meerut.

From the Editorial Casebook

I had been attending for some time a child aged three years, who had suffered primarily from convulsions, followed by vomiting and diarrhoea, with subsequent exhaustion and emaciation.

There seemed no hope of recovery, and I left my little patient one night fully believing I had seen him for the last time alive. I was late on my country rounds next day, and when I arrived at the cottage I noticed the blinds were drawn, and, upon entering, my eyes at once fell upon a couch pushed into a corner of the room, and covered by a white sheet, whilst the broken-hearted parents were weeping by the settle. I sat down and tried to comfort them, and finally left directions as to the hour when they might send for the death certificate. Before leaving I walked toward the couch, and drew back the covering from the pale waxen face. The jaw was fastened by a band in the usual way and coppers had been placed over the eyelids. As I stood looking intently at the child I fancied I detected the slightest movement of the chest. It could but be imagination, I thought; nevertheless, instinctively I felt for the wrist, but failed to detect a pulse. Still, I watched – there again was that tremor! I applied my stethoscope to the region of the heart without response, but, feeling dissatisfied, I undid the nightdress, and applied the instrument to the bare skin. I could hardly believe my ears: there was undoubtedly a beat! I shall never forget the shriek which the mother gave when I said, 'Mrs W., your child is not dead!' I at once applied hot flannels to the feet, and gently massaged the body for two or three hours, and had the satisfaction before I left – long after the undertaker had come and gone – of seeing the child taking nourishment in its mother's arms. He is now a fine, strong, healthy lad. He might have been otherwise.

An incident related at a meeting of the London Association for the Prevention of Premature Burial, 18th January 1903: a lady, living in Holland Road, Kensington, testified that on hearing the news of the loss of her property, she went into violent hysterics for two hours, and then was thought to have died. After being left for twenty-four hours, she was taken out of her bed, rolled on the floor, and needles and pins were stuck in her. Next morning one of the servants, on looking at her body on the bed, thought it moved. The doctor was sent for again, but he certified that she was undoubtedly dead, and so the coffin was ordered. Three hours afterwards her daughter said: 'I don't think mother is dead,' and applied some brandy to the cold lips.

'Then I came to,' said the lady, who added, 'That was five years ago. I have my death certificate at home! Although I could not move, I could hear everything. I heard the men take my measurement for the coffin.'

'That,' said Mr Arthur Lovell (the hon. sec.), 'was a state of trance with which I am rather familiar. What we want are State-appointed certifiers to examine all cases of supposed decease.'

The Undertakers' Journal, 22nd July 1893, says:

Charles Walker was supposed to have died suddenly at St Louis a few days ago, and a burial certificate was obtained in due course from the coroner's office. The body was lying in the coffin, and the relatives took a farewell look at the features, and withdrew as the undertaker's assistants advanced to screw down the lid. One of the undertaker's men noticed, however, that the position of the body in the coffin seemed to have undergone some slight change, and called attention to the fact.

Suddenly, without any warning, the 'corpse' sat up in the coffin and gazed round the room. A physician was summoned, restoratives were applied, and in half an hour the supposed corpse was in a warm bed, sipping weak brandy and water, and taking a lively interest in the surroundings. Heart-failure had produced a species of syncope resembling death that deceived even experts.

Syncope is not a disease but is merely a symptom of certain maladies. It is described as 'Fainting or swoon; a sudden suspension of the heart's action, accompanied by cessation of the functions of the organs of respiration, internal and external sensation, and voluntary motion.' There appears, therefore, every probability that, with careless or ignorant medical practitioners, a certificate of death may be given where there is merely a suspension and not a termination of life.

The Banner of Light, Boston, 28th July 1894, quotes the following case of apparent sudden death medically certified:

Sprakers, a village not far from Rondout, N.Y., was treated to a sensation Tuesday, 10th July, by the supposed resurrection from the dead of Miss Eleanor Markham, a young woman of respectability, who to all appearance had died on Sunday, 8th July.

Miss Markham about a fortnight ago complained of heart trouble, and was treated by Dr Howard. She grew weaker gradually, and on Sunday morning apparently breathed her last, to the great grief of her relatives, by whom she was much beloved. The doctor pronounced her dead, and furnished the usual burial certificate. On account of the warm weather it was decided that the interment should take place Tuesday, and in the morning Miss Markham was put in the coffin.

After her relatives had taken the last look on what they supposed was their beloved dead, the lid of the coffin was fastened on, and the undertaker and his assistant took it to the hearse waiting outside. As they approached the hearse a noise was heard, and the coffin was put down and opened in short order. Behold! there was poor Eleanor Markham lying on her back, her face white and contorted, and her eyes distended.

'My God!' she cried, in broken accents. 'Where am I? You are burying me alive.'

'Hush! child,' said Dr Howard, who happened to be present. 'You are all right. It is a mistake easily rectified.'

The girl was then taken into the house and placed on the bed, when she fainted. While the doctor was administering stimulating restoratives the trappings of woe were removed, and the hearse drove away with more cheerful rapidity than a hearse was ever driven before.

'I was conscious all the time you were making preparations to bury me,' she said, 'and the horror of my situation is altogether beyond description. I could hear everything that was going on, even a whisper outside the door, and although I exerted all my willpower, and made a supreme physical effort to cry out, I was powerless. At first I fancied the bearers would not hear me, but when I felt one end of the coffin falling suddenly, I knew that I had been heard.'

Miss Markham is on a fair way to recovery, and what is strange is that the flutterings of the heart that brought on her illness are gone.

Thirteen Days after 'Death'

In a letter received from Mrs H.E. Wright, of Ilford, Essex, under date 31st May 1897, she says:

The most extraordinary case I ever heard of was one related by an aged relative, which happened in a ladies' boarding-school at Edinburgh, in which she was a pupil. This must have been between eighty and ninety years ago. A young girl from the West Indies was confided in an especial manner to the care of the lady principal.

One day the girl died, after having been indisposed for a few days. The best doctors in Edinburgh, one of the chief medical schools in the world, pronounced the girl dead, and wanted to have her buried, but the principal declared that nothing on earth would induce her to have the child buried until unmistakable signs of corruption showed themselves; but days passed and no signs to satisfy the good lady appeared, who meanwhile kept applying hot bread to the soles of the feet. At last, after ten days or so, even the eminent doctors began to be staggered.

At the end of thirteen days, when the principal went to her room with hot bread, she found the girl sitting up in bed, rubbing her eyes in a somewhat bewildered manner, and expressing a desire to get up and set about her lessons. It is quite possible that had she not come from such a distance her own relations might have been called in, and the poor child buried; but in days when there were no steamers, and a voyage to the West Indies might mean two or three months, the schoolmistress felt all the agony of letting the parents know that their daughter had been dead many weeks before the information came to them. So she acted with the determination of despair, and acted wisely and well.

A Resuscitated Humorist

The Undertakers' Journal of May, 1888, narrates an interesting and apparently trustworthy story:

Mrs Lockhart, of Birkhill, who died in 1825, used to relate to her grandchildren the following anecdote of her ancestor, Sir William Lindsay, of Covington, towards the close of the seventeenth century: 'Sir William was a humorist, and noted, moreover, for preserving the picturesque appendage of a beard at a period when the fashion had long passed away. He had been extremely ill, and life was at last supposed to be extinct, though, as it afterwards turned out, he was merely in a "dead faint" or trance. The female relatives were assembled for the "chesting", the act of putting a corpse into a coffin, with the entertainment given on such melancholy occasions in a lighted chamber in the old tower of Covington, where the "bearded knight" lay stretched upon his bier.

'But when the servants were about to enter to assist at the ceremonies, Isabella Somerville, Sir William's great-granddaughter and Mrs Lockhart's grandmother, then a child, creeping close to her mother, whispered into her ear, "The beard is wagging! The beard is wagging!" Mrs Somerville, upon this, looked to the bier, and, observing indications of life in the ancient knight, made the company retire, and Sir William soon came out of his faint. Hot bottles were applied and cordials administered, and in the course of the evening he was able to converse with his family. They explained that they had believed him to be actually dead, and that arrangements had even been made for his funeral. In answer to the question, "Have the folks been warned?" (i.e., invited to the funeral) he was told that they had, that the funeral day had been fixed, an ox slain, and other preparations made for entertaining the company.

'Sir William then said, "All is as it should be; keep it a dead secret that I am in life, and let the folks come." His wishes were complied with, and the company assembled for the burial at the appointed time. After some delay, occasioned by the non-arrival of the clergyman, as was supposed, and which afforded an opportunity of discussing the merits of the deceased, the door suddenly opened, when, to their surprise and terror, in stepped the knight himself, pale in countenance and dressed in black, leaning on the arm of the minister of the parish of Covington. Having quieted their alarm and explained matters, he called upon the clergyman to conduct an act of devotion, which included thanksgiving for his recovery and escape from being buried alive. This done, the dinner succeeded. A jolly evening, after the manner of the time, was passed, Sir William himself presiding over the carousals.'

Restoration by Warmth

The Lancet, 27 November 1858, cites a remarkable case which was afterwards corroborated in all its details by the surgeon who attended the patient, Mr. R.B. Mason, of Nuneaton.

The girl, whose name is Amelia Hinks, is twelve or thirteen years of age, and resides with her parents in Bridge Street, Nuneaton. She had lately appeared to be sinking under the influence of some ill-explained disorder, and about three weeks since, as her friends imagined, she died. The body was removed to another room. It was rigid and icy cold. It was washed and laid out. The limbs were decently placed, the eyelids closed and penny-pieces laid over them. The coffin was ordered. For more than forty-eight hours the supposed corpse lay beneath the winding-sheet, when it happened that her grandfather, coming from Leamington to assist in the last mournful ceremonies, went to see the corpse. The old man removed a penny-piece, and he thought that the corpse winked! There was a convulsive movement of the lid. This greatly disturbed his composure; for, though he had heard that she died with her eyes open, he was unprepared for this palpebral signal. A surgeon is said to have been summoned, who at first treated the matter as a delusion, but subsequently ascertained stethoscopically that there was still slight cardiac pulsation.

The body was then removed to a warm room, and gradually the returning signs of animation became unequivocal. When speech was restored, the girl described many things which had taken place since her supposed death. She knew who had closed her eyes and placed the coppers thereon. She also heard the order given for her coffin, and could repeat the various remarks made over her as she lay in her death clothes. She refused food, though in a state of extreme debility. She has since shown symptoms of mania, and is now said to have relapsed into a semi-cataleptic condition.

Apparent Death in Pregnancy

Christoph Hufeland (one of the greatest authorities on the subject in Germany), in his essay upon the uncertainty of the signs of death, tells of a case of the wife of Professor Camerer, of Tübingen, who was hysterical, and had a fright in the sixth month of her pregnancy, that brought on convulsions (eclampsia), which continued for four hours, when she seemed to die completely. Two celebrated physicians, besides three others of less note, regarded the case as ended in death, as all recognised signs of death were present. However, attempts to revive her were at once resorted to, and were continued for five hours, when all the medical attendants, except one, gave the case up, and left.

The physician who remained pulled off a blister-plaster that had been put on one of the feet, when the lady gave feeble signs of life by twitchings about the mouth. The doctor then renewed his efforts to revive her, by various stimulating means, and by burning, and by pricking the spine; but all in vain, for after her slight evidences of revival, she seemed to die unmistakably. She lay in a state of apparent death for six days, but there was a small space over the heart where a little warmth could be detected by the hand, and on this account the burial was put off. On the seventh day she opened her eyes, and slowly revived, but was completely unconscious of all that had happened. She then gave birth to a dead child, and soon thereafter recovered her health completely.

Dr Frederick A. Floyer, of Mortimer, Berks, published the following case in the *Tocsin*, 1st November 1889:

> A narrow escape was recently communicated direct to the writer, and as it has some extremely important bearings on the value of what are usually considered to be evidences of death, we give it as told by the survivor, who is still alive in the form of a cheery and intelligent old lady in the fullest possession of her faculties and memory.
>
> Herself the wife of a medical officer attached to the –th Regiment, she was stationed at – Island, where at the age of twenty-eight she was safely confined. Shortly after giving birth she was walking out with an attendant when she was taken suddenly ill with a painful spasm of the heart – what appears to have been an attack of *angina pectoris* – and was conveyed indoors and propped up with pillows, suffering great pain, and although medical attendance was summoned, nothing was of avail, and she died – at least in the opinion of those around her, who paid the proper attention to what they regarded as a corpse.
>
> It was the custom there to bury at sundown anyone who died during the day. We understand that in warm countries it is difficult to close the eyelids properly, and so this lady, lying motionless and rigid, contemplated with perfectly clear perception, but with an utter indifference, the bringing in of the coffin and the necessary preparations for her interment; she remembers her children coming to take a last look at her, and then being taken downstairs.
>
> She would never have lived to tell the story but for an accident, which happened in this way. Her nurse, who was

much attached to her, was stroking her face and the muscles of her jaw, and presently declared she heard a sound of breathing. Medical assistance was summoned, and the mirror test applied, but the surface was undimmed. Then, to make sure, they opened a vein in each arm, but no blood flowed. No limb responded to stimulus, and they declared that the nurse was mistaken, and that the body was dead beyond doubt.

But the nurse persisted in her belief and in her attentions, and did succeed in establishing a sign of life. Then mustard applications to her feet and to the back of her neck, and burnt feathers applied to her nostrils, which she remembered burning her nose, completed her return to consciousness.

Archbishop's Startling Experience

The *Medical Times*, London, 1866, remarks as follows:

There may be real danger of burial before life is quite extinct. Now, we will only reproduce the cases reported by Cardinal Archbishop Donnet, in the French Senate, in a discussion on a petition that the time between death and burial should be lengthened.

His Eminence said he had the very best reasons for believing that the victims of hasty interments were more numerous than people supposed. He considered the rules and regulations prescribed by the law very judicious; but, unfortunately, they were, particularly in the country, not always executed as they should be, nor was sufficient importance attached to them. In the village he was stationed in as an assistant-curate in the first period of his sacerdotal life, he saved two persons from being buried alive. The first was an aged man, who lived twelve hours after the hour prescribed for his interment by the municipal officer; the second was a man who was quite restored to life. In both cases a trance more prolonged than usual was taken for actual death.

The *Medical Times* correspondent gives the other instances in the words of the Archbishop:

The next case that occurred to me was at Bordeaux. A young lady, who bore one of the most distinguished names in the Department, had passed through what was supposed the last agony, and, as apparently all was over, the father and mother were torn away from the heartrending spectacle. As God willed it, I happened to pass the door of the house at the moment, when it occurred to me to call and inquire how the young lady was going on. When I entered the room, the nurse, finding the body breathless, was in the act of covering the face, and, indeed, there was every appearance that life had departed. Somehow or other, it did not seem to me so certain as to the bystanders. I resolved to try. I raised my voice, called loudly upon the young lady not to give up all hope that I was come to cure her, and that I was about to pray by her side.

'You do not see me,' I said, 'but you hear what I am saying.' My presentiments were not unfounded. The word of hope I uttered reached her ear and effected a marvellous change, or, rather, called back the life that was departing. The young girl survived; she is now a wife, and mother of children, and this day is the happiness of two most respectable families.

The final incident related by the Archbishop is so interesting, and made such a sensation, that it deserves to be repeated in his own words.

In the summer of 1826, on a close summer day, in a church which was exceedingly crowded, a young priest, who was in the act of preaching, was suddenly seized with giddiness in the pulpit. The words he was uttering became indistinct; he soon lost the power of speech, and sank down on the floor. He was taken out of the church and carried home. All was thought to be over.

Some hours after, the funeral bell was tolled, and the usual preparations made for the interment. His eyesight was gone; but if he could see nothing, like the young lady I have alluded to, he could hear, and I need not say that what reached his ears was not calculated to reassure him. The doctor came, examined him, and pronounced him dead; and after the usual inquiries as to his age and the place of his birth, etc., gave permission for his interment next morning. The venerable bishop, in whose cathedral the young priest was preaching when he was seized with the fit, came to his bedside to recite the 'De Profundis'. The body was measured for the coffin.

Night came on, and you will easily feel how inexpressible was the anguish of the human being in such a situation. At last, amid the voices murmuring around him, he distinguished that of one whom he had known from infancy. That voice produced a marvellous effect and superhuman effort. Of what followed I need say no more than that the seemingly dead man stood next day in the same pulpit.

That young priest, gentlemen, is the same man who is now speaking before you, and who, more than forty years after that event, implores those in authority, not merely to watch vigilantly over the careful execution of the legal prescriptions with regard to interments, but to enact fresh ones in order to prevent the recurrence of irreparable misfortunes.

Medical Experiences

The Lancet, of 2nd June 1866, says that Dr Brewer, in the course of the address delivered to the Guardians of St George's at St James's Hall, dwelt upon the question of suspended animation in a passage which really deserves to be quoted.

> I have been more than once under a condition of apparently suspended respiration, and yet, active as is my brain, and sensitive as is my body, I remember as well as though it were but yesterday that, on being restored to consciousness, no feeling of discomfort of any kind attended my experience on either occasion.
>
> It is under the truth to say I have known a score of cases of those who have been supposed dead being reanimated. It is not many months ago a friend of mine, a rector of a suburban parish, was pronounced by his medical attendant to be dead. His bed was arranged, and the room left in its silence. His daughter had re-entered and sat at the foot, and the solemn toll of his own church bell was vibrating through the chamber, when a hand drew aside the closed curtain, and a voice came from the occupant of the bed: 'Elizabeth, my dear, what is that bell tolling for?' The daughter's response was, perhaps, an unfortunate one: '*For you, Papa.*'

Dr H.S. Tanner, in a letter in *The New York Times*, 18th January 1880, mentions two cases where persons awakened from trance at the moment of sepulture described in turn what their feelings had been. Said one:

Have you ever felt the paralysing influence of a horrible nightmare? If you have had such experience, then you are prepared to conceive of the mental agonies I endured when I realised that my friends believed me dead, and were making preparations for my burial. The hours and days of mental struggle spent in the vain endeavour to break loose from the vice-like grasp of this worse than horrible nightmare was a hell of torment such as no tongue can describe or pen portray.

Dr Johnson, of St Charles, Illinois, is the other instance mentioned by Dr Tanner, who in his hearing, and in the presence of a large audience in Harrison's Hall, Minneapolis, stated that when a young man he was prostrated with a fever. He swooned away, apparently dead. His attending physician said he was dead. His father was faithless and unbelieving, and refused to bury him. He lay in this condition, apparently dead, fourteen days. The attending physician brought other physicians to examine the apparently lifeless form, and all stated unqualifiedly, 'He is dead.' Some fourteen physicians, among them many eminent professors, examined the body, and there was no ambiguity in the expression of their conclusion that the boy was dead. But the father still turned a deaf ear to all entreaties to prepare the body for the grave.

Public feeling was at last aroused. The health officer and other city officers, acting in their official capacity, and by the advice of physicians, peremptorily demanded that the body be interred without delay. On the fourteenth day the father yielded under protest; preparations were made for the funeral, when the emotions of the still living subject, who was conscious of all transpiring around him, were so intense as to be the means of his deliverance. He awoke from his trance.

Danger In Wasting Diseases

A solicitor, living in Gloucester, recently informed us that, when first in practice, he had as caretaker of his offices an old woman who, with her husband, had been in charge of the cholera wards, erected just outside the city, at the time of the severe epidemic of 1849, when, in Gloucester alone, there were 119 fatal cases. She told him that as soon as the patients were dead they put them in shells and screwed them down, so as to get them out of the way as quickly as possible, as the small sheds (which are still standing) were so crowded.

'Sometimes,' she callously remarked, 'they come to afterwards, and we did hear 'em kicking in their coffins, but we never unscrewed 'em, 'cause we knew they'd got to die!'

Narrow Escapes In Cholera

Dr Chew communicated the two following cases during his sojourn in Calcutta in the early part of 1896.

In March, 1877, Assistant-Surgeons H.A. Borthwick, S. Blake, H.B. Rogers, and myself received orders to proceed from Rawalpindi by bullock-train to Peshawur to join the various regiments we were to be posted to for duty. We had just passed a place called Rati when Borthwick showed strong symptoms of cholera, from which he suffered all that night. The nearest hospital was twenty-five miles behind us, and though we had neither medicines nor sick-room comforts with us, we had no alternative but to journey onwards, because the bullock-train drivers refused to turn back, and if we did return to Rawalpindi we would have been court-martialled for disobeying lawful commands and coming back without orders to do so. Travelling by bullock-train is very slow work, and far from a comfortable mode of transit; however, we were obliged to make the best of it, and early next morning Borthwick was cold, stiff, and seemingly dead.

Here was a fine state of affairs. The nearest cantonment, Nowshera, which we had no expectation of reaching before nine p.m., was thirty-six miles off, and by the time we arrived, it would have been too late to approach the authorities, while Peshawur, our destination, was another twenty-nine miles further off. Dispose of the body we dare not, and we had no choice but to continue our route. All that day there was not a movement or other sign to show that life was not extinct, and affairs seemed no better by five p.m. next day, when we reached Peshawur.

The apparent corpse was lifted out of the bullock-train and carried into the hospital dispensary (where a strong fire was blazing) preparatory to papers being signed and arrangements made for its final disposal. Whether it was the heat of the fire before which he was placed, or whether the vibriones had produced an antitoxin, I am not prepared to argue; but *we do know* that Borthwick recovered consciousness while lying on the bed in that dispensary, and that he whom we mourned as dead returned to life.

The Undertakers' Journal, 22nd May 1895, has the following:

The Reverend Harry Jones, in his reminiscences, and as a London clergyman, declares his conviction that in times of panic from fatal epidemics it is not unlikely that some people are buried alive. Mr Jones recalls a case within his knowledge of a young woman pronounced to be dead from cholera, and actually laid out for the usual collecting cart to call from the undertakers, when a neighbour happened to come in and lament over her. The story continues thus: 'And is poor Sarah really dead?' she cried.

'Well,' said her mother, 'she is, and she will soon be fetched away; but if you can do anything you may do it.' Acting on this permission, the practical neighbour set about rubbing Sarah profusely with mustard. Sarah sat up, stung into renovated life, and so far recovered as to marry; 'and I myself,' says Mr Jones, 'christened four or five of her children in the course of the next few years.'

Consumption and Epilepsy

The following details are given by the Cincinnati correspondent of the *New York Herald* from Memphis, Tennessee:

Mrs Dicie Webb keeps a grocery store on Beale Street, and is well known to hundreds. Two years ago John Webb, a son of Mrs Webb, married Sarah Kelly, a pretty girl, to whom the mother-in-law became greatly attached. Before one year of their married life had passed, Mrs Webb, jun., was stricken with consumption, and on several occasions came near dying.

About a month ago the young woman became very anxious to visit her parents in Henderson County, and she was taken there. At first she appeared much improved, and hopes were felt that her life might be preserved through the summer, but two weeks ago last Tuesday a telegram announced her death, and the husband hurried to her parents' home. Three days later he returned with the corpse. Her mother-in-law pleaded so hard for a sight of the dead woman that finally, despite the belief that the body was badly decomposed, it was decided to open the coffin.

While looking at the placid face, Mrs Webb was terrified at beholding the eyelids of the dead woman slowly opening. The eyes did not have the stony stare of death, nor the intelligent gleam of life. Mrs Webb was unable to utter a sound. She could not move, but stood gazing at the gruesome sight. Her horror was increased when the supposed corpse slowly sat upright, and, in an almost inaudible voice, said, 'Oh, where am I?' At this the weeping woman screamed. Friends who rushed into the room were almost paralysed at the sight, and fled shrieking. But one bolder than the others returned and spoke to the woman, who asked to be laid on the bed. Hastily she was taken from the coffin and cared for.

In the course of the day the resurrected woman fully regained her mental powers. The day following she related a wonderful story. She said she was cognisant of all that occurred, and did not lose consciousness until she was put aboard the train for Memphis. Soon after being placed in her mother-in-law's house she came to her senses and knew all that was passing. While her mother-in-law was looking at her she made a supreme effort to speak. Mrs Webb lived a number of days, when she again apparently died. The doctors pronounced her dead, and she was once more placed in the coffin.

While the mother-in-law was taking her final farewell she heard a voice whisper, 'Mother, don't cry.' Looking into the girl's face, she saw the same look that she had noticed before. She called for help, and several women responded. Some-one cried, 'Shake her; she's not dead.' In the excitement of the moment, the women, it is thought, shook the life out of the poor consumptive, and last Saturday she was buried. The family and friends have endeavoured to keep the matter quiet.

A Strange Bit of Personal History

Dr Chew writes:

In 1873 I was a student in the Bishop's High School, Poonah, where I used to be generally at the head of my class, and when competing for the Science Prizes I was fully determined to take the first prize or none. The Reverend Mr Watson, Rector of St Mary's Church and Chaplain to our school, knew my disposition, and cautioned me against being too sanguine, lest disappointment might tell very keenly. The disappointment came, and with it much nervous excitability.

Shortly after this (Christmas 1873) my favourite sister was seized with convulsions that carried her off. From the moment of her decease to nearly a month after her interment, I entirely lost the power of speech. On the day of the funeral I was parched with thirst, but could not drink, as the water seemed to choke me. My eyes were burning and my head felt like bursting, but I could neither sob nor cry. I felt quite dazed, and followed the procession to the cemetery, where I stood motionless by the open grave; but as soon as they lowered the little coffin into its resting-place, I threw myself headlong into the grave and fainted away. Someone pulled me out and carried me home, where I lay in a sort of stupor for nine days, during which Dr Donaldson attended me most patiently, and I regained consciousness, but was too weak to even sit up in bed.

On the 16th January 1874, I felt a peculiar sensation as of something filling up my throat, with no swelling, no pain nor anything that pointed to throat affection and this getting worse and worse, in spite of everything, I *died*, as was supposed, on the 18th of January 1874, and was laid out for burial, as the most careful examination failed to show the slightest traces of life. I had been in this state for twenty hours, and in another three hours would have been closed up forever, when my eldest sister, who was leaning over the head of my coffin crying over me, declared she saw my lips move. The friends who had come to take their last look at me tried to persuade her it was only fancy, but as she persisted, Dr Donaldson was sent for to convince her that I was really dead. For some unexplained reason, he had me taken out of the coffin and examined very carefully from head to foot.

Noticing a peculiar, soft, fluctuating swelling at the base of my neck, just where the clavicles meet the sternum, he went to his brougham, came back with his case of instruments, and, before anyone could stop him or ask what he was going to do, laid open the tumour and plunged in a tracheotomy tube, when a quantity of pus escaped, and, releasing the pressure on the carotids and thyroid, was followed by a rush of blood and some movement on my part that startled the doctor. Restoratives were used, and I was slowly nursed back to life; but the tracheotomy tube (I still carry the scar) was not finally removed till September 1875.

Startling Resurrections

From *The London Echo*, 3rd March 1896:

A letter from Constantinople, in the *Politische Korrespondenz*, gives a remarkable case of an apparent death which would have ended in a premature burial but for the high ecclesiastical position of the person concerned. On the 3rd of this month, Nicephorus Glycas, the Greek-Orthodox Metropolitan of Lesbos, an old man in his eightieth year, after several days of confinement to his bed, was reported by the physician to be dead. The supposed dead bishop, in accordance with the rules of the Orthodox Church, was immediately clothed in his episcopal vestments, and placed upon the Metropolitan's throne in the great church of Methymni, where the body was exposed to the devout faithful during the day, and watched by relays of priests day and night. Crowds streamed into the church to take a last look at their venerable chief pastor.

On the second night of 'the exposition of the corpse,' the Metropolitan suddenly started up from his seat and stared round him with amazement and horror at all the panoply of death amidst which he had been seated. The priests were not less horrified when the 'dead' bishop demanded what they were doing with him. The old man had simply fallen into a death-like lethargy, which the incompetent doctors had hastily concluded to be death. He is now as hale and hearty as can well be expected from an octogenarian.

But here it is that the moral comes in. If Nicephorus Glycas had been a layman he would most certainly have been buried alive. Fortunately for him, the Canon Law of the Orthodox Church does not allow a bishop to be buried earlier than the third day after his death; whereas a layman, according to the ancient Eastern custom, is generally buried about twelve hours after death has been certified. The excitement which has been aroused by the prelate's startling resurrection may tend to set men thinking more seriously about the frequent probability of the cruel horror of the interment of living persons.

Whenever graveyards have been removed, owing to the rapid expansion of towns, in America, or examined elsewhere, unmistakable evidences of premature burial have been disclosed, as will be seen in this volume; bodies have been found turned upon their faces, the limbs contorted, with hair dishevelled, the clothing torn, the flesh mutilated, and coffins broken by the inmates in their mad endeavour to escape after returning consciousness, to terminate life only in unspeakable mental and physical agonies. It may be said that every graveyard has its traditions, but the facts are carefully concealed lest they should reach the ears of the relatives, or incriminate the doctors who had with such confidence certified to actual deaths which were only apparent.

It is not, however, the custom to remove graveyards in Europe until all possibility of such discoveries has disappeared. To reopen a grave is to break the seal of domestic grief. There is a widespread belief that where a coffin, with a duly certified corpse – dead or alive – has been screwed up, it must not be opened without an authorization from a magistrate, mayor, or other official, and many people have been suffocated in their coffins while waiting for this formality. Common sense, under the circumstances, seems to be often paralysed.

According to English Law

In England it has been decided (Reg. *v.* Sharpe) to be a misdemeanour to disinter a body without lawful authority, even where the motive of the offender was pious and laudable; and a too rigorous interpretation of this and similar enactments in other countries has led to the suffocation of many unfortunate victims of a mistaken medical diagnosis, whose lives, by prompt interposition, might have been saved.

They Waited for the Key

Koppen, in his work, entitled *Information Relative to Persons who have been Buried Alive*, Halle, 1799, quotes the following amongst a large number of cases of premature burial:

> In D –, the Baroness F – died of smallpox. She was kept in her house three days, and then put in the family vault. After a time, a noise of knocking was heard in the vault, and the voice of the Baroness was also heard. The authorities were informed; and instead of opening the door with an axe, as could have been done, the key was sent for, which took three or four hours before the messenger returned with it. On opening the vault it was found that the lady was lying on her side, with evidences of having suffered terrible agony.

They All Waited for One Another

Christian Struve, in his essay on *Suspended Animation*, 1803, relates the following:

> A beggar arrived late at night, and almost frozen to death, at a German village, and observing a schoolhouse open, resolved to sleep there. The next morning the schoolboys

found the poor man sitting motionless in the room, and hastened, affrighted, to inform the schoolmaster of what they had seen. The villagers, supposing the beggar to be dead, interred him in the evening. During the night the watchman heard a knocking in the grave, accompanied by lamentations. He gave information to the bailiff of the village, who declined to listen to his tale.

Soon afterwards the watchman returned to the grave, and again heard a hollow noise, interrupted by sighs. He once more hastened to the magistrate, earnestly soliciting him to cause the grave to be opened; but the latter, being irresolute, delayed this measure till the next morning, when he applied to the sheriff, who lived at a distance from the village, in order to obtain the necessary directions. He was, however, obliged to wait some time before an interview took place. The more judicious sheriff severely censured the magistrate for not having opened the grave on the information from the watchman, and desired him to return and cause it to be opened without delay. On his arrival, the grave was immediately opened; but, just Heaven! what a sight! The poor, wretched man, after having recovered in the grave, had expired for want of air. In his anguish and desperation he had torn the flesh from his arms. All the spectators were struck with horror at this dreadful scene.

They Waited for the Home Secretary

The Undertakers' Journal, 22nd November 1880, relates the following: 'An extraordinary story is reported from Tredegar, South Wales. A man was buried at Cefn Golan Cemetery, and it is alleged that some of those who took part in carrying the body to the burial-ground heard knocking inside the coffin. No notice was taken of the affair at the time, but it has now come up again, and the rumour has caused a painful sensation throughout the district. It is stated that application has been made to the Home Secretary for permission to exhume the body.

They Waited for the Priest

Dr Franz Hartmann, in his *Premature Burial*, relates the two following cases:

In the year 1856 a man died in an Hungarian village. It is customary there to dig the graves in rows. As the grave-digger was making the new grave he heard sounds as of knocking proceeding from a grave where a man had been buried a few days previously. Terrified, he went to the priest, and with the priest to the police. At last permission was granted to open the grave; but by that time its occupant had died in reality. The fact that he had been buried alive was made evident by the condition of the body, and by the wounds which the man had inflicted upon himself by biting his shoulders and arms.

They Waited for the Police

In a small town in Prussia, an undertaker, living within the limits of the cemetery, heard during the night cries proceeding from within a grave in which a person had been buried on the previous day. Not daring to interfere without permission, he went to the police and reported the matter. When, after a great deal of delay, the required formalities were fulfilled and permission granted to open the grave, it was found that the man had been buried alive, but that he was now dead. His body, which had been cold at the time of the funeral, was now warm and bleeding from many wounds, where he had skinned his hands and head in his struggles to free himself before suffocation made an end to his misery.

They Waited Five Hours for an Order

A medical correspondent communicates to the author particulars of the following case, which occurred at Salzburg, Austria:

> Some children were playing in the Luzergasse Cemetery, and their attention was attracted by knocking sounds in a newly made grave. They informed the gravedigger of it, and he secured permission to open the grave from whence the sounds seemed to come. A man had been buried there at two p.m. that day. The formalities of the permission to open the grave delayed it till seven p.m., when, on opening the coffin, the body was found to be bent completely over forwards, and was frightfully distorted and bleeding from places on the hands and arms, which seemed to have been gnawed by the man's own teeth. The medical experts who were called in to examine the case declared that the man had been buried alive.

They Waited for the Mayor

From *The Undertakers' Journal*, 22nd January 1887:

Another shocking case of premature burial is reported; the distressing incident took place at Saumur, in France. A young man suddenly died, at least to all appearance, and his burial was ordered to take place as soon as possible. The *croque-morts*, or undertaker's men, who carried the coffin to the grave, thought they heard a noise like knocking under its lid, yet, being afraid of creating a panic among the people who attended the funeral, they went on with their burden. The coffin was duly placed in the grave, but, as the earth was being thrown upon it, unmistakable sounds of knocking were heard by everybody. The mayor, however, had to be sent for before the coffin could be opened, and some delay occurred in the arrival of that official. When the lid was removed, the horrible discovery was made that the unfortunate inmate had only just died from asphyxia.

They Waited for the Local Authorities

From *The Star*, London, 13th May 1895:

A woman who was believed to have died the day before was being buried at Doussard, France, when the gravedigger, who was engaged in filling up the grave, distinctly heard knocking coming from the coffin. He called a man who was working near, and he came and listened, and heard the knocking also. It was then about nine o'clock in the morning. The knocking continued, and they listened for about half an hour, when it occurred to one of them that they ought to do something, so they went to inform the local authorities. The *curé* of the village was the first to arrive on the scene; but as no one had any authority to exhume the body, the coffin was not taken up. All that was done was to bore some holes in the lid with a drill in such a way as to admit of air.

By midday all the necessary formalities had been gone through, and it was decided at last to open the coffin. This was done; but whether the unfortunate woman was still alive at this time is doubtful. Some of those present affirm that she was. They state that they saw a little colour come into her cheeks, and the eyes open and shut. One thing is certain, viz., that when at half-past six in the evening it was finally decided to consult a doctor, the practitioner summoned declared that death had taken place not more than five or six hours before. It was thought that had the coffin been opened directly the sounds were heard, the woman's life might have been saved, and she would have been spared hours of indescribable torture and suffering.

They Waited but Were Prompt

The Paris edition of the *New York Herald*, 14th May 1895, says:

A woman, belonging to a village near Limoges, died, to all appearance at least, a few days ago. After the body had been placed in a coffin, it was transported to the village church. On the way the bearers heard sounds proceeding from it, and at once sent for the mayor, who ordered it to be opened.

The woman was found to be suffering from *eclampsia*, which had been mistaken for death by her relatives.

When will people learn to exercise common sense, and remember that life is more valuable than red tape, and the spirit of human pity and practical sympathy of greater moment than the lettter of the law?

CHAPTER 7:
BURIAL OF DOUBTFUL CASES

There is a great and natural reluctance on the part of medical practitioners to admit that they have made mistakes in death certification, particularly in any one of the various forms of death counterfeits, or suspended animation. It should be noted that amongst the lectures delivered on special occasions, such as the opening of the medical schools, the subjects of trance and the danger of premature burial are conspicuous by their absence; allusion to these subjects is of rare occurrence, nor does the study of this abstruse branch of medicine, so far as can be ascertained, form part of any medical curriculum.

Many medical men do not believe in death-trance. They declare that they have never seen such a case, and in their judgement, when a sick patient ceases to breathe, when volition is suspended, and the stethoscope reveals no signs of cardiac action, the death is real, and the case beyond recovery. But the reader will already have gathered, from the results of inquiry in many countries disclosed in the foregoing pages, that such evidence is not in itself sufficient to justify the risk of possible live sepulture. There should be no sign, nor any collection of signs, deemed of sufficient weight, apart from the process of decomposition.

Was She Dead?

As an instance of the justifiable uneasiness caused by the neglect of this simple precaution, we quote from the *Medical Times*, London, 1860:

A lady entering upon the ninth month of pregnancy died of pneumonia. All the other phenomena of death ensued, except that the colour of the face was unusually lifelike. On the fifteenth day from that of death there was not the least cadaveric odour from the corpse, nor had its appearance much altered, and it was only on the sixteenth day that the lips darkened. The temperature of the atmosphere had undergone many changes during the time mentioned, but although there had been frost for a short period, the weather was in general damp and cold.

This lady may have been dead, but she may not. What we maintain is that the burial laws should have been such as to make it certain that she was dead before interment, by the appearance of general decomposition. And it must be obvious to the least reflective reader that in countries where burial follows quickly upon supposed death (as in Turkey, France and Italy, some parts of Ireland and throughout India), or where there is no compulsory examination of the dead (as in the United States or the United Kingdom), and amongst people like the Jews (since Jewish custom enjoins speedy interment), and especially in cases of sudden death (where attempts at resuscitation are rare), the number of premature burials may be considerable.

CHAPTER 8:
CAUSES OF DEATH-COUNTERFEITS

In *Premature Burial* Dr Hartmann says:

> In 1866, in Kronstadt, a young and strong man, Orrendo
> by name, had a fit and died. He was put into a coffin and
> deposited in the family vault in a church. Fourteen years
> afterwards, in 1880, the same vault was opened again for the
> purpose of admitting another corpse. A horrible sight met
> those who entered. Orrendo's coffin was empty, and his
> skeleton lying upon the floor. But the rest of the coffins were
> also broken open and emptied of their contents. It seemed
> to show that the man after awakening had burst his coffin
> open, and, becoming insane, had smashed the others, after
> which he had been starved to death.

Cerebral Concussion

Dr Brouardel, Professor of Medical Jurisprudence, Paris,
mentions a case which came under his own eyes while he was
house-physician at La Pitié. He says:

> A little bricklayer, aged thirteen, was brought in one day,
> who had fallen from the sixth story to the pavement. The
> boy had been taken to a chemist, who pronounced him
> to be dead, and sent him on to the hospital. The director
> refused to admit him, as he was dead. Now, either by intu-
> ition or else to bamboozle the director, I stated that the lad
> was alive, although sounds of the heart could not be heard.

I had him put into a mustard bath, and, to my delight, he came to. He had received no wound, nor any definite injury, only he remembered nothing.

The writer adds, 'He might have been buried alive.'

Various Predisposing Diseases

Living burials take place because the general public are ignorant of the fact that there are many (some thirty) diseases, and some states of the body that cannot be called diseases, as well as a number of incidents and accidents, which produce all the appearances of death so closely as to deceive anyone. Excessive joy or excessive grief will often paralyse the nervous system, including the action of the heart and the respiratory functions, and occasion the appearance of sudden death; as well as shocks, blows upon the head, fright, strokes of lightning, violent displays of temper; also certain drugs now in common medical use, such as Indian hemp, digitalis, tobacco, morphia, and veratrum. According to Dr Léonce Lenormand, in *Des Inhumations Précipitées*, the following diseases and conditions not infrequently produce the like symptoms, viz., apoplexy, asphyxia, catalepsy, epilepsy, nervous exhaustion, ecstasy, haemorrhage, hysteria, lethargy, syncope, tetanus, etc.

CHAPTER 9:
THE TOWERS OF SILENCE

Superstitions and Dangers

Mr Nasarvariji F. Billimoria, in a communication dated 14th March 1896, says that where cases of premature burning have occurred in India, the relatives are unwilling to have the facts published, and shrink from making them known. Moreover, when persons have been once declared dead, and have been rejected by their friends while in the land of shadows, and have returned to this life, they are believed to bring misfortune with them, and discredit is attached to the families in consequence. Mr Billimoria says the following cases can be relied upon as authentic.

In the year 18– , in the town of B– , a Marwari[6] was taken as dead, and carried to the cremation-ground. Unfortunately, at that time a superstition was prevalent among all classes of Indians that, if a dead one is brought back to his or her house, a plague would break out in the town. When, therefore, the Marwari survived, instead of bringing him back to the house, or even allowing him to roam elsewhere, he was killed, it is said, by a hatchet, which they were in the habit of carrying with them to break the fuel for the funeral pyre. This had happened in the old days when governments did not interfere in the superstitious customs of the people.

Fortunately, however, those days are gone, and with them the old superstitions. Some time ago a fisherwoman, after taking a liberal dose of alcoholic drink and opium, was found (apparently) dead by her relatives, low-caste Hindus.

No time is lost among the Hindus, high or low caste, to remove the body to the cremation ground after a man is found dead.

A bamboo bier was being prepared to carry the fisherwoman to the cremation ground, upon which the body was laid as usual, and the relatives were to lift it to their shoulders: when, lo! the woman turned herself on the bier on her side, and, thanks to the good sense of the fisherman, she is still enjoying her life while I am writing.

A young daughter of a Bania was sick for a long time, and was found apparently dead by her relatives, and carried to the cremation ground. These are generally situated at a riverside. When the bier was prepared for certain ceremonies, the girl showed signs of revival, and, one by one, the relatives would go near the bier, bend down, stare at the face, and retire aghast. Information had reached the town that the girl had survived; but the body, nevertheless, was cremated, and never brought back to the house. It is believed that in this case, although the girl had revived for a little time, she had died soon afterwards, as she had been ill for a long time previously. Granting that this was a case in which the dying became actively conscious a few minutes before real death, it is certain that great and indecent haste was practised by the relatives in pressing on with the cremation, as is the usual mode in India.

Canine Diagnosticians

Another custom amongst the Parsees in the treatment of their dead is to bring a dog to the corpse before it is removed from the house, and another dog on its arrival at the Tower of Silence.

This ceremony is known as the Sagdeed. The explanation is that, according to the ancient belief, the spotted dog can discriminate between the really and the apparently dead. Dr Franz Hartmann and other writers appear also to be of the opinion, which the author considers highly probable, that a dog knows whether his master is really dead or only in a trance; but that a strange dog would be able to discriminate and act as a sentinel to prevent a living person being mistaken for a dead one, is highly improbable.

Instances of Canine Sagacity

The Parsee custom of using the dog is suggestive. There are numerous cases on record where a dog, following his master to the grave as one of the mourners, has refused to leave the grave; and these have been quoted as a proof of the undying love of the master's canine friend. May it not be that dogs are gifted, as believed by the Parsees, with another sense denied to most men, the faculty of discerning between real and apparent death?

A medical correspondent relates the following:

In Austria, in 1870, a man seemed to be dead, and was placed in a coffin. After the usual three days of watching over the supposed corpse, the funeral was commenced; and when the coffin was being carried out of the house, it was noticed that the dog which belonged to the supposed defunct became very cross, and manifested great eagerness towards the coffin, and could not be driven away. Finally, as the coffin was about to be placed in the hearse, the dog attacked the bearers so furiously that they dropped it on the ground; and in the shock the lid was broken off, and the man inside awoke from his lethargic condition, and soon recovered his full consciousness. He was alive and well at last news of him. Dogs might possibly be of use in deciding doubtful cases, where their master was concerned.

Also the following:

The postmaster of a village in Moravia 'died' in a fit of epilepsy, and was buried three days afterwards in due form. He had a little pet dog which showed great affection towards him, and after the burial the dog remained upon the man's grave and howled dismally, and would not be driven away. Several times the dog was taken home forcibly, but whenever it could escape it immediately returned. This lasted for a week, and became the talk of the village.

About a year afterwards that part of the graveyard had to be removed owing to an enlargement in building the church, and consequently the grave of the postmaster was opened, and the body was found in such a state and position as to leave no doubt that he had been buried alive, had returned to consciousness, and had died in the grave. The physician who had signed the certificate of death went insane on that account, soon after the discovery was made.

CHAPTER 10:
THE DANGER OF HASTY BURIALS

Early burials are advocated and defended by certain writers on sanitary grounds; and there is, no doubt, something to be said for them, provided the body shows unmistakable signs of dissolution. However, to impose a general rule of speedy burial upon Englishmen by Parliament, or upon Americans by State Legislature, as has been urged, would but add to the existing evil of perfunctory and mistaken diagnosis of death, and greatly increase the number of premature interments.

Ancient Practices

Plato enjoined the bodies of the dead to be kept until the third day, *in order to be satisfied of the reality of the death.* The Romans kept the bodies of the dead a week before burial, lest through haste they should inter them while life remained. Servius, in his commentary on Virgil, tells us 'that on the eighth day they burned the body, and on the ninth put its ashes in the grave'. Quintilian explains why the Romans delayed burials as follows: 'Because we have seen persons return to life after they were about to be laid in the grave as dead.'

Danger of Jewish Custom

In all countries it is the custom amongst the Jews to bury their dead, and apparently dead, quickly, without taking the slightest steps for restoration, and many are the catastrophes recorded.

The *Jewish World*, 13th September 1895, observes:

Cases of trance and of the burial of persons who only seemed to be dead, and of narrow escapes of others from the most terrible of all imaginable fates, are not so uncommon as most people suppose; and while Jews adhere to the practice of interring their dead within a few hours after their supposed demise, there will always be a risk of such horrible catastrophes happening, even more frequently among us than among the general community. So strict is the Jewish Law as regards the risk of destroying life, that it is prohibited to even move or touch a man or woman who is on the point of death, lest we hasten, by a moment, their dissolution.

Jewish Catastrophes

The *British Medical Journal*, 8th March 1879, under the heading of 'Suspended Animation', relates the following incident:

A Jew, aged seventy, who had been ailing for some time, apparently died recently in Lemberg, on a Friday night, after severe convulsions. The decease having been legally certified, the body was put on a bier, preparatory to the funeral, which had to be deferred, the next day being the Jewish Sabbath. Two pious brethren who had, according to their custom, been spending the night in prayer, watching the dead, were suddenly, on the morning of the

Saturday, disturbed from their devotions by strange sounds proceeding from the bier, and, to their dismay, saw the dead man slowly rising, and preparing to descend from it, using at the same time very strong language. Both brethren fled very precipitately; and one of them has since died from the effects of the fright.

The Lancet's Trenchant Criticism

The Lancet, 23rd August 1884, comments thus upon the subject of 'Burying Cholera Patients Alive':

> It is not so much undue haste as inexcusable carelessness that must be blamed for the premature burying of persons who are not really dead. Let it be once for all decided that measures shall be taken to ascertain the fact of death before burial. Why not revert to the old practice, and always open a vein in the arm after death, or pass a current of electricity through the body before the coffin is finally screwed down? It may be held that these unpleasant resorts are unnecessary. We do not think they are.

The Danger is Real

It must be remembered that in the rural districts nothing in the shape of examination to establish the fact of death is practised; while in certain parts of Cornwall, throughout the greater part of agricultural Ireland, amongst the Jews in all cities and towns, as well as those who in all places are certified as having died of cholera, smallpox, and other infectious and epidemic diseases, burial often follows certified death quite as quickly as in the Continental states. In all the public resorts on the Continent the hotel-keepers, through an insensate fear of death and the injury which the possession of 'a corpse', dead or alive, may do to their business, have them coffined and disposed of, particularly in the night, within a few hours of their supposed death. These scandalous homicidal acts are of everyday occurrence, and the rapacious landlords have no difficulty in obtaining certificates of death from the accommodating *mort verificateurs*.

CHAPTER 11:
FEAR OF PREMATURE BURIAL

Demonstrated by Wills

Many of those who are most familiar with the phenomena of life and death have left precise instructions in their wills for various preventives which experience has shown to be necessary, so as to make sure that they shall not be subjected, like thousands of human beings, to the unspeakable horrors of being buried alive. Several daily papers drew attention to the will of Miss Caroline Townsend Robarts, of Bromley, Kent, in which the testatrix desired that on her death a medical man should cut an artery or apply some other means to ascertain that death was certain, and to avoid the danger of her being buried in a trance.

Peculiar Requests

Mr Horace Welby, in his volume entitled *Mysteries of Life, Death, and Futurity*, 1861, says: 'Francis Douce, the antiquary, requested, in his will, that Sir Anthony Carlisle, the surgeon, should sever his head from his body, or take out his heart, to prevent the return of vitality.'

The late Lady Burton, widow of Sir Richard Burton, provided that her heart was to be pierced with a needle, and her body to be submitted to a post-mortem examination, and afterwards embalmed (not stuffed). Lady Burton, it is said, had been subject to fits of trance on more than one occasion, and was terribly afraid that such an attack might be diagnosed as death.

Harriet Martineau left her doctor ten pounds to see that her head was amputated before burial. The dread of being buried alive dictated a clause in the will of the distinguished actress, the late Miss Ada Cavendish, for the severance of the jugular vein; and prompted the late Mr Edmund Yates to leave similar instructions, with the provision that a fee of twenty guineas should be paid for the operation, which was carried out. Mr John Rose, of New York, who died in November 1895, made known his earnest desire, that his coffin should not be closed, but laid in the family vault at Roseton, and guarded day and night by two caretakers, who were instructed to watch for signs of re-animation.

A well-known and eccentric Dublin doctor, Dr Heron, was found dead in his bed at Monkstown in October 1901, and pinned to the bed over his body was the following note, written in pencil: 'Notice. Do not bury me till I am dead. Don't mind the doctors, unless they put a knife through my heart. You will never forgive yourselves. No mortal can tell if a man is dead until he begins to rot, or there is a good hole through his head.' Evidence at the inquest showed that poison was taken in darkness in mistake for a sleeping draught, and a verdict of 'death from misadventure' was returned.

Corroboration by The Lancet

The Lancet, 17th March 1886, says:

> There are many apparently trustworthy stories afloat, both in this country and on the Continent, which favour the belief

that premature interment is really of not so unfrequent occurrence as might be supposed. Some few have actually made provision in their wills that means should be taken, by cutting off a finger, or making a pectoral incision, etc., to excite sensibility after their supposed death; whilst a French countess left a legacy to her medical attendant as a fee for his severance of the carotid artery in her body before it was committed to the tomb.

Public Testimonies

In a lecture delivered at Everett Hall, Brooklyn, New York, June 1883, Mr J.D. Beugless, the then President of the New York Cremation Society, said that an undertaker in that city (Brooklyn) recently made provision in his will, and exacted a promise from his wife of great caution, that his body should be cremated, being induced thereto by the fear of being buried alive.

'Live burials,' he says, 'are far more frequent than most people think.' It is reported that another undertaker of Brooklyn some time since deposited a body in a receiving vault temporarily: when he went some days later to remove it for burial, what was his horror, to find the body crouching at the door, stark in death, the hair dishevelled, the flesh of the arms lacerated and torn, and the face having the most appalling expression of horror and despair ever witnessed by mortal eyes!

CHAPTER 12: SUDDEN DEATH

Popular Fallacy

The idea commonly entertained is that with animal bodies there are only two possible conditions – either life or death; that the presence of one of these conditions implies the absence of the other; that when the body has assumed the appearance of death, as during the sudden suspension of all the functional activities, it must be dead. This last is far from being true; for all the appearances of death are fallacious, especially those that accompany so-called sudden death. All such cases should be challenged as of doubtful character, and held so till recovery or putrefaction of the tissues proves the presence of life or of death. Popularly, we say that 'the thread of life is snapped asunder', or it is 'the going out of life', like the sudden extinguishing of a candle. Experience, however, teaches that life leaves the body in a gradual manner, and that death approaches, and takes the place of life, in one part or organ after another, thus creeping through the tissues and sometimes defying all tests to prove its presence, leaving putrefaction to be its only sign. There can be no such thing as veritable sudden death, unless the body is crushed into a shapeless mass, like an insect under foot.

The Possibility of Error

Thus, it is clear that the process of death, or the departure of life, may require days or weeks for its completion; and it may even be delayed to a time when putrefaction has set in quite generally, as when the hair and nails grow after the body has been buried some weeks, as has been credibly reported. Unfortunately there is nothing in the external appearance of those cases of so-called sudden death in which the vital machinery may be totally wrecked, to distinguish them from those of apparent death, in which all the organism is in a state of perfect integrity, and in which resuscitation is possible, provided the vital principle has not entirely left the body. Consequently, the only safe rule to observe in all cases in which death has not followed poisoning, or injuries which kill outright, or some known disease of sufficient duration and severity to bring on dissolution, is to wait for unmistakable evidences of decomposition before autopsy, embalming, cremation or burial is allowed.

Much Taken for Granted

Nothing is more common, on opening a newspaper, than to see one or more announcements of sudden death. These occurrences are so frequent that the great London dailies, except when an inquest is held, or when the deceased is a person of note, omit to record them. The narratives are much alike: the person, described to be in his usual health, is seized with faintness in the midst of his daily avocation, and he falls down apparently dead; or he retires for the night, and is found dead in his bed.

In many instances post-mortems are made and an inquest held; but in other cases the opinion of the attendant doctor, that the death is clue to heart-disease, syncope, asphyxia, coma, apoplexy or 'natural causes' is deemed sufficient. The friends who are called in to look at the body will remark, 'how natural and how life-like', 'how flexible the limbs', 'how placid the face'; and, without the faintest attempt at resuscitation, arrangements are made for an early burial.

Dr Wilder's Views

Dr Alexander Wilder, Professor of Physiology and Psychology, says: 'There are a variety of causes for sudden death. The use of tobacco is one. Another is overtaxed nervous system. I would choose such a death if I could be sure it was death. But most of those things may cause a death which is only apparent!'

French Report and English Criticism

Dr Alfred Swaine Taylor, in his standard work on Medical Jurisprudence, writes of a petition presented to the French Chamber of Deputies, wherein the petitioner declared he had known six interments of living persons to have taken place within a period of eight months. Of forty-six cases notified as being at risk of premature burial, twenty-one persons returned to life at the time they were about to be deposited in the earth, nine recovered owing to the affectionate attentions of their relations, four from the accidental falling of the coffins, two from a feeling of suffocation in their coffins, three from the puncture of pins in fastening the shrouds, and seven from unusual delay in the funerals. But, as to the 'negligence of French officials manifested by these statements', the English author of *The Principles and Practice of Medical Jurisprudence* may be reminded that not even an 'official' is held responsible for attestation of death in this country, and that probably nine-tenths of the medical certificates of death in Great Britain are given without the certifier ever personally satisfying himself by a visit of the reality of the alleged death.

Legally 'Dead', But Still Living

The Medical Times, 1859, has the following:

We find in an account taken from *The Boston Medical and Surgical Journal* some observations on the heart of a hanged criminal, which are remarkable in a moral point of view, as well as in their scientific aspect. The man died, it appears, as the phrase is, without a struggle; and, therefore, probably in the first instance he fell into a syncope. The lungs and brain were found normal. Seven minutes after suspension, the heart's sounds were distinctly heard, its pulsations being one hundred a minute; two minutes later they were ninety-eight; and in three minutes sixty, and very feeble. In two minutes more the sounds became inaudible.

The man was suspended at ten o'clock, and his body was cut down twenty-five minutes afterwards. There was then neither sound nor impulse. At 10.40 the cord was relaxed, and then the face became gradually pale; the spinal cord was uninjured. At 11.30 a regular movement of pulsation was observed in the right subclavian vein; and, on applying the ear to the chest, there was heard a regular, distinct, and single beat, accompanied with a slight impulse.

Hereupon Drs Clark, Ellis, and Shaw open the thorax, and expose the heart, which still continues to beat! The right auricle contracted and dilated with energy and regularity.

At twelve o'clock the pulsations were forty in a minute; at 1.45 five per minute. They ceased at 2.45; but irritability did not entirely disappear until 3.18, more than five hours after suspension.

CHAPTER 12: SIGNS OF DEATH

No one sign is in itself sufficient proof of death, unless it be that of putrefaction. It is rather by a combination of signs that the fact may be ascertained prior to the putrefaction stage; but how far the investigator may be misled will be seen in the following pages.

Popular Fallacy

There exists a common belief that if breathing and pulsation cease for only a brief period it will be impossible for consciousness to be recovered, and a trifling experiment, such as feeling the pulse at the wrist, or holding a mirror to the face, is sufficient to create the belief in the popular mind that death has really taken place. But whilst it would appear presumptuous to attempt to doubt or deny a theory so widely accepted by both the lay and medical world, yet numerous well-attested facts conclusively show that such vital actions may be suspended, and may even resist the most rigorous tests known to science, only to be followed by the recovery of the sleeper.

The Mobility Test

It has been deemed a sure sign of death, when for a considerable period no physical movement takes place; and also when the lower jaw falls directly afterwards. However, many physical changes may take place *after* death consequent upon muscular contraction or relaxation, as well as by the generation of gases; and the jaw may be fixed as in strychnine poisoning.

The Respiratory Test

This is perhaps the least satisfactory test, the custom of holding a mirror before the mouth being quite untrustworthy. The most practised eye is apt to be deceived.

Heart and Circulation Test

The pulses of the body, as well as the movements and sounds of the heart, may be undetectable at a time when the body is not only not dead but actually recoverable. In cases of catalepsy the respiratory muscles have not been seen to move, yet inspiration and expiration however slowly and imperceptibly must have taken place.

Rigor Mortis Test

Rigor mortis is a condition that seldom or never supervenes in the hot weather in India, and is often a feature of catalepsy.

The Diaphanous Test

The diaphanous test consists in taking a hand of a supposed dead person, placing it before a strong artificial light, with the fingers extended and just touching each other, and then looking through the narrow spaces between the fingers to see if there be a scarlet line of light. The theory is that if there be such a line of scarlet colour there is some circulation still in progress. However, Sir Benjamin Ward Richardson has reported an instance in which the test, applied to the hand of a lady who had simply fainted, gave no evidence of the red line; she therefore, on that test alone, might have been declared dead. He was once summoned to another case in which the reverse was presented; the body was dead, whilst the red line supposed to indicate life was perfectly visible.

The Putrefaction Test

There is but one really trustworthy proof that death has occurred in any given instance, viz., the presence of a manifest sign of commencing decomposition. This condition is always ascertainable, at all events to the professional eye, and it should always be verified before a certificate of death is signed.

Precautions in Württemberg

In the Royal Decree issued by the Government for examining the dead in Württemberg, dated 24th January 1882, various signs and experiments for enabling the official inspector to ascertain if actual death has taken place are laid down. Among these are:

(1)   The cessation of sensibility may be assumed if, on raising the eyelid, the pupil remains unaltered when a lighted

candle is held close to it; or if pungent odours, such as those derived from onions, vinegar, volatile ammonia, or by severe friction of the chest, arms, or soles of the feet, the application of mustard, or burning tinder, or if sealing-wax dropped upon the chest produces no reaction, and particularly if in the latter case the skin does not blister.

(2)   The stoppage of the circulation of the blood, apart from the absence of heart-beating, if, after tying a tight bandage around the arm, the veins do not swell up, upon the hands being firmly gripped; also if, upon pricking the lips, no blood escapes.

In most of the continental states there are state-appointed surgeons to examine the dead, *medecins verificateurs*, and in some of these, Württemberg, for instance, the official is obliged to examine the corpse several times before his certificate is made out. But notwithstanding this careful official inspection, cases of premature burial and narrow escapes are telegraphed every now and then to the English press.

The Danger of Haste

Mr Clarke Irvine, who has had a wide experience, writing in *The Banner of Light*, 14th December 1895, Boston, U.S., says:

How many have passed underground forever, of whom nothing was ever suspected! All through the country people are dying or apparently dying, or falling into death-like trances daily, and being placed in their coffins as a matter of course, and hurried to and into their graves. Hundreds upon hundreds have been and are being consigned to that most awful of all the dooms possible. The horror of the thing is simply unspeakable.

Extracts from the Police Instructions in Bavaria as to Corpse Inspection of 20th November, 1885.

Indications of death may be noted:

If there is no indication of any pulsation noticeable.

If the eyelids when pulled asunder remain open, and the eyes themselves appear sunken into their sockets, dulled, and lustreless, also if the eyeballs feel soft and relaxed.

If parts of the body are pale and cold, if chin and nose are pointed, if cheeks and temples are sunken.

If a feather or burning candle held against the mouth shows no sign of motion, or if there is no sign of moisture upon a looking-glass held before the mouth.

If on different parts of the body, particularly the neck, back, or posterior, or the undersurface of the extremities, there are bluish-red spots (death spots) visible.

If the skin, particularly at the sides of the stomach, shows a dirty-green discolouration (decomposition spots).

If the inspection gives rise to suspicions of apparent death, the inspector must adopt the necessary measures for resuscitation, as follows:

Opening of the windows, and warming the room.

Efforts at artificial respiration.

Applications of warm mustard-plaisters to the chest and the extremities.

Rubbing with soft brushes, with cloths saturated in vinegar or spirit of camphor.

Irritation of the throat with a feather.

CHAPTER 14:
DURATION OF DEATH-COUNTERFEITS

The differences observed in the length of time that persons have remained in this condition depended, doubtless, upon the constitutional peculiarities of the patients such as strength or weakness or upon the nature of the disease from which they may have suffered. Hence children and young persons will endure longer than the aged. Also upon the nature of the element in which the accident happened, whether it contained greater or less proportion of oxygenated or carbonic acid gas, or other poisonous vapours.

A. Josat, in *De la Mort et de ses Caractères*, gives the result of his own observations in one hundred and sixty-two instances, in which apparent death lasted:

In 7 cases from 36 to 42 hours
In 20 cases from 20 to 36 hours
In 47 cases from 15 to 20 hours
In 58 cases from 8 to 15 hours
In 30 cases from 2 to 8 hours

The order of frequency of diseases in which these occurred was as follows: asphyxia, hysteria, apoplexy, narcotism, concussion of the brain, the cases of concussion being the shortest.

A person buried while in a state of trance, catalepsy, asphyxia, narcotism, nervous shock, etc., and in any of the other states that cause apparent death without passing through a course of disease, will have a longer struggle before life becomes extinct than one whose strength had been exhausted by an attack of sickness.

Dr Charles Londe, in his *La Mort Apparente*, remarks:

It has been calculated that, after one quarter of the quantity of atmospheric air contained in the coffin (approximately estimated at 120 litres) was exhausted, death would set in; therefore it is quite certain that, if the shroud is thick, and the coffin well closed, and the grave impenetrable to the atmosphere, life could not last more than forty to sixty minutes after inhumation. But is not that a century of torture?

Some allowance should be made for the persistence of the vital energy, which continues after all atmospheric air is cut off.

Experiments on dogs show that the average duration of the respiratory movements after the animal has been deprived of air is 4 mins, 5 secs. The duration of the heart's action is 7 mins, 11 secs. The average of the heart's action, after the animal has ceased to make respiratory efforts, is 3 mins, 14 secs. These experiments further showed that a dog may be deprived of air during 3 mins, 50 secs, and afterwards recover without the application of artificial means.

Prof. P. Brouardel, in *La Mort et la Mort Subite*, observes that: 'A dog, placed in a common coffin, lived five to six hours; but a dog occupies less room than a man, who, in such a coffin, when closed, would not have more than one hundred litres, so he would possibly live twenty minutes. I would not wish anybody to pass twenty such cruel minutes.'

Historical Cases of Live Burial

In a volume entitled *Information Relative to Persons who have been Buried Alive*, dedicated to Frederick William III, King of Prussia, are the following amongst many other cases:

Medical Professor Junker, in Halle, a very humane man, had a corpse of a suicide by hanging delivered for dissection at his college. He was placed on a table in the dissecting room, and covered with a cloth. About midnight, while the professor was sitting at his writing-table in an adjoining room, he heard a great noise in the dissecting room, and, fearing that cats were gnawing at the corpses, he went out, and saw the cloth in a disturbed condition, and on lifting it up found the corpse missing. As all the doors and windows were closed, he searched the room, and found the missing one crouching in a corner, trembling with cold, in the terror of death. He besought the professor for mercy, help, and means for escape, as he was a deserter from the army, and he would be severely punished if caught. After consideration, the kind professor clothed him, and took him out of town at night as his own servant, passing the guards pretending to be on a professional visit, and set him free in the country. Years afterwards he met the same man in Hamburg as a prosperous merchant.

Various Statistical Estimates

Professor Froriép says that 'In 1829, arrangements were made at the cemetery, New York, to bury the corpses in such manner as not to prevent them communicating with the outside world, in case any should have awakened to life; and among 1,200 persons buried six came to life again.' In Holland, the same author states, of a thousand cases investigated, five came to life before burial, or at the grave. The Rev. J.G. Ouseley, in his pamphlet on *Earth to Earth Burial*, London, 1895, estimates that 'Two thousand seven hundred persons at least, in England and Wales, are yearly consigned to a living death, the most horrible conceivable.'

The Revd Walter Whiter, in *A Dissertation on the Disorder of Death*, 1819, calls attention to one of the reports where the following passage occurs:

Monsieur Thieurey, Doctor Regent of the Faculty of Paris, is of opinion that one-third, or perhaps half, of those who die in their beds are not actually dead when they are buried. He does not mean to say that so great a number would be restored to life. In the intermediate state, which reaches from the instant of apparent death to that of total extinction of life, the body is not insensible to the treatment it receives, though unable to give any signs of sensibility.

Dr Léonce Lenormand, in his able treatise, *Des Inhumations Précipitées*, has given his deliberate opinion that a thousandth part of the human race have been, and are, annually buried alive.

A Medical Man's Caution

The following appears in *The Lancet*, 14th June 1884:

Sir, That this is an incident that does happen, and frequently has happened, has for some years past been my firm conviction; and during epidemics, particularly in the East, its possible contingency has frequently caused me much anxiety; and when the burial has, for sanitary reasons, had to be very hurried, I always made it a rule to withhold my certificate, unless I had personally inspected the body and assured myself of the fact of death.

The reason and necessity for extreme caution in such matters were impressed vividly upon me some years ago, when visiting the crypt of the cathedral at Bordeaux, where two bodies were shown, to whom, I think it obvious, this most terrible of all occurrences must have happened; and I am unable to attribute the position in which they were found in their coffins, and the look of horror which their faces still displayed, to any action of rigor mortis or any other post-mortem change, but simply and solely to their having awakened to a full appreciation of their most awful position.

In the case of one of these bodies, which was found lying on its side, the legs were drawn up nearly to a level with the abdomen, and the arms were in such a position as to convey the impression that both they and the legs had been used in a desperate, but futile, attempt to push out the side of the coffin; whilst the look of horror remaining on the face was simply indescribable. In the other case, the body was found lying on its face, the arms extended above the head, as if attempting to push out the top of the coffin. In the year 1870 these two bodies were still on view; and the attendants used to dwell at some length upon the horrors of being interred alive.

It appears that some years prior to 1870, in making excavations in a churchyard in the immediate vicinity of the cathedral, the workmen came upon a belt of ground that apparently was impregnated with some antiseptic material, as all the bodies within this belt, to the number of about two hundred, were found to be almost as perfect as when they were buried; of these a selection appears to have been made; and at the time I mention about thirty or forty were exhibited, propped up on iron frames, in the crypt of the cathedral. The impression left on my mind at the time was, that if out of two hundred bodies so discovered there could be two in which, to say the least, there is a strong probability of live interment, this awful possibility was a thing that should receive more attention than is generally devoted to it. I am, sir, your obedient servant,

H.S.

Conditions in France

M. Gaubert, in *Les Chambres Mortuaires d'Attente*, Paris, 1895, says that in France there are in round numbers 36,000 communes, and it is beyond doubt that in every one of these will be found cases of premature burial. Communes with a population of eight hundred even have several. Dr Pineau has recorded twelve in the single commune of Fontenay-le-Comte in Poitou. M. Gaubert declares that he would not be far from the truth in estimating the number of victims to apparent death at 8,000 a year. Dr Josat, lauréat de l'Institut, declares that a considerable number of people refuse to visit France through fear that they might be overtaken by apparent death and precipitately buried alive.

CHAPTER 16:
EMBALMING AND DISSECTIONS

Embalming is no doubt preferable to the risks, prevailing in almost all countries, of burial before careful medical examination, for the reason that it is better to be killed outright by the embalmer's poisonous injections, or even to come to life under the scalpel of the anatomist, than to recover underground. A leading New York investigator has openly declared his belief that a considerable number of human beings (supposed by their relatives to be dead, but who are really only in a state of death-trance) are annually killed in America by the embalming process.

The late Miss Frances Power Cobbe was so impressed by the fear of being buried alive that she preferred being killed outright by the surgeon's knife, rather than run the risk she so much dreaded. Consequently, her will contained the following solemn injunction to her medical adviser, which was duly carried out by one of the authors of this work:

> To perform on my body the operation of completely and thoroughly severing the arteries of the neck and windpipe, nearly severing the head altogether, so as to make any revival in the grave absolutely impossible. If this operation be not performed, and its completion witnessed by one or other of my executors, and testified by the same, I pronounce all bequests in this will to be null and void.

The Risks of Embalming

F. Kempner, in *Denkschrift*, says:

> Owing to some great mental excitement, the Cardinal Spinosa fell into a state of apparent death. He was declared to be dead by his physicians, and they proceeded to open his chest for the purpose of embalming his body. When the lungs were laid open, the heart began to beat again; the Cardinal returned to consciousness, and was just able to grasp the knife of the surgeon, when he fell back and died in reality.

The *Journal de Rouen*, 5th August 1837, relates the following:

> Cardinal Somaglia was seized with a severe illness, from extreme grief; he fell into a state of syncope, which lasted so long that the persons around him thought him dead. Preparations were instantly made to embalm his body, before the putrefactive process should commence, in order that he might be placed in a leaden coffin, in the family vault. The operator had scarcely penetrated into his chest, when the heart was seen to beat. The unfortunate patient, who was returning to his senses at that moment, had still sufficient strength to push away the knife of the surgeon, but too late, for the lung had been mortally wounded, and the patient died in a most lamentable manner.

Dr Hartmann in *Premature Burial* says: 'The celebrated actress Mlle. Rachel died at Paris, on 4th January 1858. After the process of embalming her body had already begun, she awoke from her trance, but died ten hours afterwards owing to the injuries that had been inflicted upon her.'

Andreas Vesalius, successively first physician to Charles the Fifth and his son Philip the Second of Spain, being persuaded that a certain Spanish gentleman, whom he had under management, was dead, asked liberty of his friends to lay open his body. His request being granted, he no sooner plunged his dissecting-knife in the body than he observed signs of life in it, since, upon opening the breast, he saw the heart palpitating. The friends of the deceased, horrified by the accident, pursued Vesalius as a murderer; and the judges inclined that he should suffer as such. By the entreaties of the King of Spain, he was rescued from the threatening danger, on condition that he would expiate his crime by undertaking a voyage to the Holy Land.

The account of an accident that befell another anatomist is taken from the Venetian physician Terilli.

A lady of distinction in Spain, being seized with an hysteric suffocation so violent that she was thought irretrievably dead, her friends employed a celebrated anatomist to lay open her body to discover the cause of her death. Upon the second stroke of the knife she was roused from her disorder, and exhibited evident signs of life by her lamentable shrieks extorted by the fatal instrument. This melancholy spectacle struck the bystanders with so much consternation and horror that the anatomist, now no less condemned and abhorred than before applauded and extolled, was forthwith obliged to quit not only the town but also the province in which the guiltless tragedy was acted. But though he quitted the now disagreeable scene of the accident, a groundless remorse preyed upon his soul, till at last a fatal melancholy put an end to his life.

Dr Franz Hartmann, in his *Premature Burial*, has the following:

In May 1864, a man died very suddenly at a hospital in the State of New York, and as the doctors could not explain the cause of the death they resolved upon a post-mortem examination, but when they made the first cut with the knife, the supposed dead man jumped up and grasped the doctor's throat. The doctor was terrified, and died of apoplexy on the spot, but the 'dead' man recovered fully.

Brigade-Surgeon W. Curran, in his eighth paper, entitled 'Buried Alive', relates the following:

At the Medical College at Calcutta, on 1st February 1861, the body of a Hindu male, about twenty-five years of age, was brought from the police hospital for dissection. It was brought to the dissecting room about six a.m., and the arteries were injected with arsenical solution at about seven.

At eleven the prosector opened the thorax and abdomen for the purpose of dissecting the sympathetic nerve. At noon Mr Macnamara distinctly saw the heart beating; there was a regular rhythmical vermicular action of the right auricle and ventricle. The pericardium was open, the heart being freely exposed, and lying to the left in its natural position. The heart's action, although regular, was very weak and slow. The left auricle was also in action, but the left ventricle was contracted and rigid, and apparently motionless. These spontaneous contractions continued till about 12.45 p.m., and, further, the right side of this organ contracted on the application of a stimulus, such as the point of a scalpel, etc., for a quarter of an hour longer.

Bruhier, in his *Dissertation sur l'Incertitude des Signes de la Mort et l'Abus des Enterrements*, records a number of cases of the supposed dead, who, after burial, were revived at the dissecting table, together with fifty-three that awoke in their coffins before being buried, fifty-two persons actually buried alive, and seventy-two other cases of apparent death. This was at a time when body-snatching was in vogue, and it is a curious comment on our civilization to be compelled to admit that a subject of trance or catalepsy during the eighteenth or the early part of the last century had a better chance of escape from so terrible a fate than now, when the vocation of the resurrection-man has become obsolete.

Parliamentary Inquiry

A Select Committee of the House of Commons was appointed on 27th March 1893, to inquire into the subject of death certification in the United Kingdom. It was shown that in about four per cent of the cases the cause of death was ill-defined and unspecified, many practitioners having forms specially printed for their own use, in which all mention of medical attendance was omitted, the object being to enable the doctor to give certificates in cases which he has never attended. Numerous deaths attended by unqualified practitioners were certified by qualified practitioners who had probably never seen the cases; and deaths were certified by medical practitioners who had not seen the patient for weeks or months prior to death, and who knew only by hearsay of the deaths having occurred.

Remarkable evidence was produced as to the reckless mode of death certification. One medical witness testified that he saw a certificate of death, signed by a registered medical practitioner, giving both the fact and the cause of death of a man who was actually alive at the time, and who lived four days afterwards, with facts of even a more startling character described as 'murder made easy'.

It was pointed out that fraud and irregularity in giving false declarations of death are by no means infrequent. From the Registrar-General's report for England and Wales for the year 1892, it was shown that in 15,000 cases of death no inquiry had been made as to its cause, and that no certificate had been obtained from any source for a number amounting to nearly three per cent of the total returned for the year. On the same authority it appeared that in 25,000 more, or four and a half per cent, the cases were so inadequately certified as not to be classifiable, making together a class of seven and a half per cent, in which no evidence of any value as to the cause of death existed.

The necessity of carefully examining an alleged dead body before giving a certificate is illustrated by the following singular case, reported in *The Times* of 19th January 1878:

A poor woman lay very ill in her scantily furnished home in Sheffield. The doctor was sent for, and came. He at once saw that hers was a very grave case, and that she had, as he thought, little chance of recovery, even if she could get the nourishment her illness required. As he was about to leave, the question was put, 'When should we send for you again, doctor?'

'Well,' was the reply, as he looked at the poor woman and then at her wretched surroundings, 'I don't think you need send for me again. She cannot possibly get better; and to save you further trouble I'll just write you out a certificate for her burial.' And he did. After the doctor departed the woman – women always *were* wilful – got better rapidly. She has now completely recovered, and goes about carrying her burial certificate with her.'

Conditions in France

Dr Léonce Lenormand accuses the *médecins des morts* in France with culpable carelessness in the exercise of their function, which consists in verifying the reality of the death.

Instead of making a minute examination of the body to ascertain the fact of death, they are content (except in cases of death from violence) to merely glance at the body, and immediately hand the family the necessary authorisation for interment. The inspector knows that if he examined every part of the body, as in duty bound, he would be accused of barbarism and profanation. In France, in spite of *médecins vérificateurs*, probably more premature burials occur than in any country in Europe, except Turkey, immediate burial after real or apparent death being the inexorable rule.

Incident in Württemburg

A Royal Decree promulgated by the King of Württemburg provides that, immediately after a death, the body must under no circumstances be interfered with, and must not be removed from the deathbed until the authorized inspection has clearly established the fact of death. The only case of the danger of premature burial that has come to our notice in Württemburg is related by Bouchut, in his *Signes de la Mort*:

In the village of Achen, in Württemburg, Mrs Eva Meyers, twenty-three years of age, was taken ill during an epidemic. Her condition became rapidly worse, and she apparently died. They put her into a coffin, and carried her from the warm into a cold room, there to await burial, which was to take place at two p.m. on the following day. Shortly after noon on that day, and before the carriers arrived, she awoke and made an effort to rise. Her aunt, who was present, and who believed that a ghost had taken possession of her, took a stick and would have killed her, if she had not been prevented by another woman.

Nevertheless, she succeeded in pushing the body back violently into the coffin, after which she indignantly went to her room. The patient remained helplessly in that condition, and would have been buried if the usual hour for the burial had not for some reason been changed. Thus she remained for another twelve hours, when she was able to gather sufficient strength to arise. She still lives, and has paid the charges for her funeral, which were claimed by the clergy, the bell-ringer, and the undertaker.

Unreliability of Death Signs

That the risk of premature burial is not an imaginary one has been shown by the citation in this volume of cases of death-like trance which have baffled the ablest of medical experts. The painful reality is also shown by the multitude of prevent-ive measures suggested by the ingenious contrivances of those who have made this distressing subject one of patient and laborious research.

Tests of the Senses

From time immemorial it has been the custom in the East, and even in some parts of the Continent, to place women around a dead man's bed to cry and howl for the purpose of awaking him should he be only apparently dead. Similarly, not only the auditory but the olfactory nerves have been submitted to attack, by holding beneath the nose the strongest and most offensive substances. Pricking the skin with sharp instruments has also been adopted, and one savant, Josat by name, obtained first prize at the Academy of France for the invention of a pair of clawed forceps for pinching the nipples of the supposed dead, and this method held premier place as a means of distin-guishing real from apparent death until it was demonstrated that subjects under profound hysteria were as indifferent to this painfully acute process as the dead. Even the eye has been studied with a view to establishing a definite conclusion: a plan, which created some stir at the time of its announcement, consisted in photographing the retina of the eye immediately after supposed death, which, it was asserted, retained an image of the object last gazed upon. But this, and the preceding tests affecting the senses, have proved to be fallacious.

The Blister Test

A good deal of importance has been attached to the difference between a blister raised during life and one produced after death. Mr George T. Angell, the editor of *Our Dumb Animals*, Boston, U.S., whose father was pronounced by his physician dead, and returned to consciousness after preparations for the funeral had been made, has repeatedly alluded to the subject in his paper, and published preventive suggestions at various times, including one from a physician, who, having been called to a man who had been dead twenty-four hours, lighted a match and applied it to the end of one of the fingers of the corpse, when a blister was formed, and, restoratives being applied, the man recovered. The physician adds the following conclusion: 'If you are alive you cannot burn your hand without raising a blister; if you were dead, and flames should come in contact with any part of your body, no blister would appear, and the flesh would be burned.'

However, a burn may raise a blister in a dead body soon after actual death. The blister test is one which has so repeatedly failed that it cannot be relied upon.

The stethoscope, which is regarded by many medical practitioners as an infallible means of preventing premature burial, has proved a broken reed in hundreds of cases, and can be of use only when applied with other tests. Dr Roger S. Chew, February 1896:

I recollect an instance of death from cobra-bite, when, though decomposition had set in, the relatives refused to believe she was dead, because one of them declared that, though he did not see her chest rise and fall, he had distinctly heard her sigh. A medical man was called in, applied the stethoscope over her thorax, and declared he could hear sounds from her lungs.

So far he was right, but as the girl had already been dead some fourteen hours, and the weather was warm, the sounds he heard were those of the escape of the putrefactive gases bubbling upward, and unable to find an exit, as her mouth was closed with a chin-bandage, and her nostrils plugged with mucus. To convince the parents that the girl was really dead, I offered to perform artificial respiration, to which end I untied the bandage, prized open her jaws, and pressed heavily on her thorax, when some of the imprisoned gases escaped, emitting an abominable odour that brought conviction of the girl being beyond all hope.

In another case, that of my son, aged two years, after a series of brain symptoms and severe convulsions preceding an outbreak of confluent small-pox, the stethoscope told me, and a medical friend who was present, that my little boy had ceased to exist; but a liberal application of ice to his head and cardiac region, together with violent friction and artificial respiration vigorously employed for forty minutes, restored the child to me, and I thanked God that I had refused to accept the evidence of the stethoscope as final.

The Electricity Test

The application of the electric current is a powerful restorative agent in cases of suspended animation, if judiciously applied. When Ruben Korff invented his coil it was urged by many that a coil might be kept in every church in order to test each body before the funeral ceremony was proceeded with. Sir B.W. Richardson attached comparatively great importance to this test, but it must be remembered that electric excitability will last for some time after death until rigor mortis sets in.

Struve in his essay, *Suspended Animation*, under the heading of 'Apparent Death From a Fall', says:

A girl, three years of age, fell from a window two storeys high upon the pavement. Though she was considered as lifeless, Mr Squires, a natural philosopher, applied electricity. Almost twenty minutes elapsed before the shocks produced any effect. At last, when some of the electric force pervaded the breast, he observed a slight motion of the heart. The child soon after began to breathe and groan with great difficulty, and after some minutes a vomiting ensued. For a few days the patient remained in a state of stupefaction, but in the course of a week she was perfectly restored to health.

Mr E.E. Carpmael, of the Medical Department, Berkeley University, U.S.A., recommends the injection of strychnine in 'a supposed corpse', which, no doubt, would prevent live sepulture, by killing the cataleptic subject.

The most remarkable of the hypodermic injections is that of Dr S. Icard of Marseilles, who claims to have discovered an infallible test for distinguishing between persons actually or only apparently dead. The fluid he uses consists of a weak solution of Fluorescine.

If this solution, it is alleged, be injected under the skin of a living person, in two minutes the skin is strongly coloured, and the body has the appearance of suffering from an attack of acute jaundice. The whole of the eyes is said to assume a clear green tinge, the pupil almost disappears, and the eye looks as if it were a brilliant emerald set in the face. But in the case of a dead man the solution produces no effect.

The following extracts from an instructive but apparently forgotten article in Dickens' *All the Year Round*, July 1869, afford valuable suggestions:

M. de Parville now announces the possibility of a self-acting apparatus, which would declare not only whether the death be real, but *would leave in the hands of the experimenter a proof of the reality of the death.* The scheme is this: It is well known that atropine – the active principle of belladonna – possesses the property of considerably dilating the pupil of the eye. M. le Docteur Bouchut has shown that atropine has no action on the pupil when death is real. Consequently the enlargement of the pupil is a certain sign that death is only apparent.

Imagine a little camera obscura, scarcely so big as an opera-glass, containing a slip of photographic paper, which is kept unrolling for five-and-twenty or thirty minutes by means of clockwork. The apparatus, placed a short distance in front of the dead person's eye, will depict on the paper the pupil of the eye, which will have been previously moistened with a few drops of atropine. It is evident that, as the paper slides before the eye of the corpse, if the pupil dilate, its photographic image will be dilated; if, on the contrary, it remains unchanged, the image will retain its original size. An inspection of the paper then enables the experimenter to read upon it whether the death is real or apparent only.

CHAPTER 19:
COUNT KARNICE-KARNICKI'S INVENTION

The Origin of The Idea

We have devoted a special chapter to the consideration of Count Karnicé-Karnicki's ingenious invention, which has attracted so much attention on the Continent that many thousands of persons in France have left instructions in their wills for this scheme to be adopted at their interment, and a society is already formed in the United States for furthering the use of the system.

The Count is a Russian nobleman, the Chamberlain to the Tsar and Doctor of the Law Faculty of the University of Louvain. He was first aroused to the horror of premature burial when attending the funeral of a young Belgian girl, who was awakened out of her lethargy by the first shovelfuls of earth thrown upon her coffin after being lowered into the grave, and her piteous screams have haunted him ever since.

For the prevention of such tragic occurrences, he set himself the task of providing some simple means which would be within the reach of rich and poor alike.

The Apparatus Described

Broadly speaking, it consists of a long tube, about three and a half inches diameter, and a hermetically-sealed box. The tube is fixed into an aperture in the coffin as soon as the latter is lowered into the grave. No gases can escape from the tomb into the outer air, as the metallic box into which the upper end of the tube enters cannot be opened from the outside. On the chest of the supposed dead body is placed a glass ball, several inches in diameter, attached to a spring which communicates through the tube with an iron box above ground.

On the slightest movement of the chest wall, as in the act of marked breathing, or movement of the body, the glass ball releases a spring which causes the lid of the iron box to fly open immediately, thus admitting both air and light to the coffin. At the same time a flag rises perpendicularly about four feet above the ground, and a bell is set ringing which continues for about half an hour. In front of the box, an electric lamp burns which gives light after sunset to the coffin below. The tube acts also as a speaking tube, and the voice of the inmate of the coffin, however feeble, is intensified.

The working ability of the apparatus has been tested by its application to individuals who volunteered to be coffined, and who found that the mere act of breathing was sufficient to produce all the phenomena mentioned above. The price of the complete apparatus is exceedingly reasonable, only about twelve shillings; and it is suggested, in order that the very poorest may have the advantage of this simple safeguard, that authorities should keep a supply for hiring out, and putting to each coffin for at least a fortnight.

CHAPTER 20:
WAITING MORTUARIES

Of all the various methods that have been suggested or introduced for the prevention of premature interment, none has been attended with such satisfactory results as the erection of mortuaries in Germany. 'Waiting mortuaries' have existed at Munich since the beginning of the last century.

In an immense room, closed by large glass doors, through which the interior can be seen from the outside, are ranged in three rows twenty sarcophagi, fixed in a sloping position. The slabs upon which they rest are supplied with a zinc trench, filled with an antiseptic fluid. At the head of each coffin a rod is fixed, from which falls a cord having a metal ring at its extremity. This cord communicates with a system of bells, and the least pressure on the rope sets it in motion.

From the moment of its arrival at the mortuary the coffin is uncovered, and placed on one of the slabs. The body is raised, and reclines upon a cushion, and the whole is covered by a profusion of flowers, usually allowing only the head of the corpse to be seen, besides a large ticket bearing the number of identification. The hands are crossed upon the breast, and one of the fingers inserted in the ring. All this is carried out by public servants, who usually show good taste in these funeral arrangements. Many families have their dead photographed like this; and the coffin is carried into a court specially kept for this purpose. Owing to the perfect ventilation and the steadiness of the temperature, no odour is noticed but the smell of the flowers and the lighted candles. There is a room for the rich and another for the poor, adjoining each other. Nothing distinguishes them, except perhaps the quality of the flowers provided for the respective classes. The cost is very moderate. The body remains exposed thus from forty-eight to seventy-two hours. The relatives are allowed to visit, and, also, they may appoint a nun or other person to watch.

Between the two mortuaries is the caretaker's room, a narrow cell, containing the bell apparatus, which is enclosed in a long cupboard, like the case of a grandfather's clock. For furniture a table, a chair, and a couch. Windows look into the mortuary. It is here that the caretaker passes the greater part of his existence. He has to make frequent rounds of inspection, and is not allowed to leave under any pretext whatever, no matter for how short a time, unless he leaves a substitute.

In the evening he stretches himself upon his couch, where the slightest tinkle of the bell would arouse him. This frequently happens; the warning bell is so sensitive that the least shake of the corpse sets it in motion. But the guardian is not at all flustered; various causes may agitate the bell, and the waking of a corpse is a very rare occurrence. Nevertheless, the caretaker at once goes to ascertain the cause of the alarm, and, having assured himself that the corpse preserves all the signs of death, he readjusts the cord, and returns to continue his sleep. The coffin is closed only a few minutes before interment, and after a final medical examination has taken place. Sometimes, when a nervous family wishes it, the coffin is carried into a separate room, where it is kept open one or two days longer, often even making an incision on the heel.

One sad exception, however, to the usual satisfactory results at Munich is recorded by M. Gaubert in his work, *Les Chambres Mortuaires d'Attente*:

A little child, five years old, was carried to the mortuary, and the corpse was deposited as usual. The next morning a servant from the mortuary knocked at the mother's house, carrying a large bundle in his arms. It was the resuscitated child, which she was mourning as lost. The transports of joy she experienced were so great that she fell down dead. The child came to life in the mortuary by itself, and when the keeper saw it, it was playing with the white roses which had been placed on its shroud.

'A Berlin apothecary wrote to me lately,' says Dr Lenormand, 'to the effect that, during an interval of two and a half years, ten people stated to be dead had been recalled to life. I shall quote only the following: In the middle of the night the bell of the vestibule rang violently. The caretaker, who had only entered on duties within a few days, much startled, ran towards the mortuary. As soon as he opened the door he found himself confronted with one of 'the corpses' enveloped in his shroud, who had quitted his bier and was making his way out. He was a soldier of the guard believed to be dead, and he was able to join his regiment five days later.'

Dr Josat said that, during his sojourn in Germany, Herr Schmill, director of the mortuary at Frankfurt, related to him a case of apparent death which occurred under his own eyes.

In the year 1840, a girl of nineteen years died of acute pleuro-pneumonia. Her body, during very hot weather, was exposed in the mortuary for a period of eight days in a state of perfect preservation. Her face retained its colour, the limbs were supple, and the substance of the cornea transparent, whereas in ordinary cases decomposition shows itself on the third day. The parents could not reconcile themselves to have their daughter buried, and found themselves much troubled. Finally, on the ninth day, the supposed dead suddenly awoke, without any premonitory indications of life.

Belgium

M. Gaubert, a very painstaking authority, in *Les Chambres Mortuaires d'Attente*, says:

There was a case at Brussels in January, 1867, of a person who returned to life just as the bearers arrived at the mortuary. He was a workman had fallen ill, and in a few days died. This suddenness of the death caused doubts as to its reality, and after the usual delay he was taken to the mortuary connected with the cemetery. The body was to be left for a few days' observation. As soon as they arrived a noise escaped from the coffin, and arrested the attention of the people present. At once they hastened towards the coffin, and tried to restore him, and in a short time he came to life. The same evening he was able to return to his home. On the following day he went himself to the authorities to annul the record of his supposed death.

United States of America

Dr J.M. Duncan, of Kansas City, U.S.A., in an instructive article in *Medical Brief*, August 1897, relates the following remarkable experiences:

In 1865 I was on duty in a United States field hospital. On 15th May a soldier in one of the hospitals died. His body was bathed, prepared and carried to the mortuary. At daybreak next morning he was found sitting upright, was taken back to the ward, and made a good recovery. This soldier said that while the nurses were dressing him he tried to kick them, and in every way tried to make them know he was not dead; but could not move. All night, as he lay in the dead-house, he kept trying to break the spell, realising fully that he must get a move on him or be buried alive next day. He distinctly heard everything as usual, could see things before him, and his sense of feeling was perfectly normal. As twilight began to appear in the east, he was feeling chilly and felt like sneezing, in the effort of which he caught his breath, and raised himself up.

CHAPTER 21: CONCLUSION

It has been our endeavour to present in a concise form the salient facts connected with the important subject which forms the title of this work. We herewith append a summary of the chief points we have presented, and which we have sought to substantiate as far as the limited space will allow:

(1) Death-counterfeits. That trance, catalepsy, and other forms of death-counterfeit, arising from exhausting illnesses and diseases, from loss of blood and various nervous derangements, from extreme conditions of temperature, drugs, drowning, stillbirth, etc., are of such mysterious and deceptive character that we are led to the conclusion that they may easily be mistaken for real death.

(2) Tragic Results. That mistakes of this nature have occurred in numerous instances. That not only have persons been buried alive, as proved by subsequent exhumations, but that in many instances, in this and other countries, many have revived after having been supposed to be dead by their relatives and attendant physicians.

(3) Justifiable Fear. That a natural dread exists in the minds of many persons lest they should fall victims to such a terrible mistake. That the dread has been further shown by the several inventions, such as safety coffins and safety graves, which have been seized upon by the public in the hope of protecting them from the most awful of all deaths.

(4) Legal Hindrances. That the formalities associated with the disinterment of a body, or even the opening of a coffin, are fraught with dangerous possibilities to the living and to the apparently dead.

(5) Special Risks. That the risk of premature burial is especially serious in France, in Spain and Portugal, in the west of Ireland, in both European and Asiatic Turkey, and in India; also among the Jews, where both the Jewish law and ancient custom enjoin burial within a few hours of death, and for similar reasons in all oriental countries, and in the Southern States of North America.

(6) Illusory Nature of Death Signs. That the various signs which are supposed to indicate death are illusory; the only safe and infallible test of dissolution being the manifestation of putrefaction in the abdomen.

(7) Death Certificates. That the present method of granting a death certificate in this country is most unsatisfactory, seeing that the medical attendant is relieved from the necessity of viewing the supposed dead before giving it, and that every year some 10,000 death certificates are accepted by the Registrar-General in which the cause of death is not even stated.

(8) Definite Medical Training. That there should be systematic medical instruction upon the phenomena of trance, catalepsy, syncope, and other forms of suspended animation.

(9) A Real Danger. That, in view of the numerous authentic instances of premature burial, these instances can but represent large numbers of other cases which have never been brought to light.

(10) Other Risks. That even embalming, dissecting, and cremation are each and all accompanied by risks to life unless the precaution is first taken of ascertaining that life has really ceased to exist.

(11) The Only Real Safeguard. That no evidence of death is really satisfactory except that which is supplied by putrefaction, usually evidenced by the change of colour in the abdomen. That to ensure this safeguard 'waiting mortuaries' should be erected by every authority at public expense, furnished with every appliance for resuscitation, watched by qualified attendants, and in telephonic communication with a medical superintendent.

(12) An Appeal. The need for immediate action is urgent and imperative, and the prompt intervention of Parliament should be at once invoked. It is not an academic question, but one of the gravest practical character, the earnest consideration and treatment of which cannot be neglected with impunity.

NOTES

1. Founder, with Henry Olcott, of the esoteric Theosopical Society
2. Skirmisher
3. Paramedics
4. Ambulance men
5. Common grave
6. Inhabitant of North-West India

BIOGRAPHICAL NOTES

William Tebb was born on 22nd October 1830. Tebb was an entrepreneur and social reformer who supported a number of varying causes during his life including the Vegetarian Society, the United States Abolition movement, the RSPCA and the campaign to repeal the Vaccination Act. He also co-founded the Royal Normal College for the Blind. His will specified that 'unmistakeable evidence of decomposition' must be visible; he was cremated a week after his death in 1917.

Colonel Edward Perry Vollum was an American army doctor. He himself experienced a state of 'suspended animation' after nearly drowning and is credited with rescuing several people who had been given up for dead. Vollum and Tebb, were among the founders of the London Association for the Prevention of Premature Burial. He died in 1902.

Walter Robert Hadwen was born in Woolwich on 3rd August 1854. Having started his career in London as a pharmacist, Hadwen subsequently trained as a doctor. He became president of the British Union for the Abolition of Vivisection and was a notorious critic of vaccination and the germ theory of disease. He died in 1932.

Jonathan Sale is a British journalist. He was Features Editor for *Punch* magazine and writes for the *Guardian* and the *Independent*.

HESPERUS PRESS

Hesperus Press is committed to bringing near what is far – far both in space and time. Works written by the greatest authors, and unjustly neglected or simply little known in the English-speaking world, are made accessible through new translations and a completely fresh editorial approach. Through these classic works, the reader is introduced to the greatest writers from all times and all cultures.

For more information on Hesperus Press, please visit our website: **www.hesperuspress.com**